TRANSNATIONAL BUSINESS AND CORPORATE CULTURE

PROBLEMS AND OPPORTUNITIES

edited by

STUART BRUCHEY
ALLAN NEVINS PROFESSOR EMERITUS
COLUMBIA UNIVERSITY

T0347592

THE INTERNATIONALIZATION OF U.S. FRANCHISING SYSTEMS

ILAN ALON

Routledge
Taylor & Francis Group

LONDON AND NEW YORK

First published 1999 by Garland Publishing, Inc.

2 Park Square, Milton Park, Abingdon, Oxon OX14 4RN
711 Third Avenue, New York, NY 10017, USA

First issued in paperback 2016

Routledge is an imprint of the Taylor & Francis Group, an informa business

Library of Congress Cataloging-in-Publication Data
Alon, Ilan.

    The internationalization of U.S. franchising systems / Ilan Alon.

       p. cm. — (Transnational business and corporate culture)
    Revision of the author's thesis (Ph.D.—Kent State University).
    Includes bibliographical references and index.

    ISBN-13: 978-0-8153-3387-6 (hbk)
    ISBN-13: 978-1-1389-7311-4 (pbk)

    1. Franchises (Retail trade)—United States. I. Title. II. Series.
HF5429.235.U5A38 1999
381'.0973—dc21   99-36253

To Anna

Contents

List of Tables   ix
List of Figures   xi
Preface   xiii
Acknowledgments   xv

Chapter I. Introduction to the Study   3

   Introduction   3
   Statement of Purpose   4
   Importance of the Study   4
   Research Design   6
   Scope of the Study   7
   Methodology   7
   Organization of this Study   8

Chapter II. Literature of International Franchising   11

   Introduction   11
   International Franchising Definitions   12
   Theories of International Franchising   14
   Conclusion   24

Chapter III. The Model   25

   Introduction to Model Development   25
   The Model   26
   Conclusion   34

Chapter IV. Research Design   37

    Introduction the Methodology   37
    Methodology   38
    Conclusion   45

Chapter V. Data Analysis   47

    Introduction   47
    Retail Sector Analysis   48
    Hotel and Motel Sector Analysis   54
    Professional Business Services Analysis   58
    Conclusion   65

Chapter VI. Summary and Conclusions   67

    Introduction   67
    Comparisons of the Hypotheses   67
    Managerial Implications   75
    Conclusions   76
    Future Research   77

Bibliography   81
Index   91
About the Author   93

List of Tables

Table 2.1   Country Factors Influencing International Franchising   17

Table 3.1   Summary of Variables and Hypotheses   33

Table 4.1   Measurement of the Variables and Hypotheses   42

Table 5.1   Descriptive Statistics and Correlations for the Retail Sector   50

Table 5.2   The Retail Logistical Model   51

Table 5.3   Descriptive Statistics and Correlations for the Hotel and Motel Sector   55

Table 5.4   The Hotel and Motel Logistical Model   56

Table 5.5   Descriptive Statistics and Correlations for the Professional Business Service Sector   61

Table 5.6   The Professional Business Services Logistical Model   62

Table 6.1   Comparisons of the Three Industries   68

Table 6.2   Descriptive Statistics and Correlations for All Three Industries   73

Table 6.3   Logistical Model for All Three Industries   74

List of Figures

Figure 2.1 A Paradigm of International Franchising   15
Figure 3.1 The Model: Organizational Model of
            International Franchising   35

Preface

The growth in the internationalization of franchising systems in the United States is undeniable. By the year 2005, it is estimated that most US franchising systems will have international outlets. The internationalization of franchising systems in the United States has been attributed to push and pull factors originating within and outside the franchising firms. Among the pull factors are the emergence of (1) multinational regional trading areas such as the North American Free Trade Agreement (NAFTA) and the European Union (EU), (2) newly industrialized countries in East Asia and Latin America, and (3) democratic and capitalistic reforms in transition economies such as Hungary, Poland and the Czech Republic.

While these external factors explain the general trend of internationalization among US based franchisors, they do not explain why some franchisors within the same industry internationalize while others prefer to operate solely in the domestic environment. Despite the opportunities abroad, domestic franchisors need to consider their institutional constraints and resources. The aim of this book is to examine in detail the factors which have led franchisors to seek international franchisees. The focus is on organizational factors since the environmental factors are similar within each of the studied industries. The scope of the analysis includes three industries: (1) Retailing, (2) Hotels and Motels, and (3) Professional Business Services.

The book makes two major contributions to international franchising theory. First, it shows that organizational factors, including size, age, growth rate, price bonding, and dispersion, explain why some franchisors within a proposed industry internationalize. The results largely support the overall argument of the book: resources and monitoring capabilities drive the internationalization of franchising systems. The second contribution of the book is the finding that the impact of organizational variables on the decision to internationalize is industry specific.

While this book targets an academic audience, this book can be extremely useful to practitioners as well, particularly in the studied industries. For example, for all of the studied industries, the number of outlets in the system was a significant factor of internationalization. The finding suggests that franchisors must reach a certain scale before attempting to internationalize. Early internationalization can be detrimental to profits and may discourage future efforts. The optimal size necessary for internationalization, however, may be industry specific.

Ilan Alon
State University of New York
May 1999

Acknowledgments

This book is the end product of several years of research on the topic of international franchising. The conception, writing and editing of this book demand the acknowledgment of many people and organizations who were involved in various stages of manuscript development.

This book started out as a dissertation submitted to the Kent State University Graduate School of Management in partial fulfillment of the requirements for the degree of Doctor of Philosophy in Business Administration. The author, therefore, wishes to acknowledge the significant contributions of the dissertation committee which included Dr. David McKee (Chairperson), Dr. Donald Williams, Dr. Kathy Wilson and Dr. John Ryans. Dr. McKee, in particular, was extremely helpful in all the stages of dissertation development.

The book breaks down the explanation of international franchising into three industries: (1) Retailing, (2) Hotels and Motels, and (3) Professional Business Services. Sections from this book pertaining to the latter two industries have been published previously by two journals. *The Journal of Global Business* (10 (18) 55-62) published the article entitled "The Organizational Determinants of the Internationalization of Franchising Systems in the Hotel Sector." *The Journal of Consumer Marketing* (6 (1) 74-85) featured the article "The Internationalization of Professional Business Service Franchises," (co-authored with Dr. David McKee). The author is grateful for their permission to republish the results associated with two of the mentioned industries.

The author also wants to thank the useful suggestions brought up by the conference participants of the Association of Marketing Theory and Practice (1997), International Academy of Business Studies (1998),

International Society of Franchising (1999), and International Management Development Association World Business Congress (1999).

Most importantly, I would like to thank my parents for standing by me, encouraging me, and supporting me through hard times. The achievements of my entire life I owe all to them.

The Internationalization of U.S. Franchising Systems

CHAPTER I

Introduction to the Study

INTRODUCTION

Franchising is a growing method of doing business both domestically and internationally. It started in the United States in the early 1900s, but did not gain acceptance throughout the world until the 1960s. In the late 1960s and early 1970s, the internationalization of the US franchise system began (Welch 1989). In 1971, 156 US franchisors operated under 3500 outlets globally (Kostecka 1988); this compares with 354 US franchisors operating over 31,000 outlets in 1986 (Kostecka 1988). In 1988, 17 percent of US franchisors had more than 35,000 outlets in international markets (Falbe and Dandridge 1992). Aydin and Kacker (1990) estimated that foreign outlets of international franchisors have increased at a rate of 17 percent per year. This trend of growth is expected to continue (Shane 1996b, Fladmoe-Lindquist 1996).

Franchising and services go hand in hand (Cross and Walker 1987). Restaurants, educational services, car rental services, business aids, and retailing are only a few services in which franchising prevails. Much of the domestic retail industry is franchised, accounting for about $900 million a year in sales, approximately 40 percent of all retail sales (Rubel 1995). Cross and Walker (1987) maintained that the growth in the domestic service sector paralleled the growth in domestic franchising because of the match between franchising attributes and service marketing problems. This is because franchising solved some of the problems associated with services. Intangibility is lessened through differentiated signs, logos, atmosphere, and other tangibles. Heterogeneity of the service and efficiency are controlled through standards and procedures. Finally, satisfaction is maximized via centralized marketing that creates consistent expectations.

Welch (1989) contended that international franchisors require that the host country have a large service sector. Root (1987) argued that international expansion through franchising is very attractive to service and retailing firms because it allows the service provider to enter with low levels of financial involvement and risk. This was true in the international expansion strategy of Marks & Spencer. Whitehead (1991, p. 11) reported that "for Marks & Spencer the advantages of franchising are that it allows the company the opportunity to expand its global presence, and establish the St. Michael name in new markets, with minimal capital investment."

STATEMENT OF PURPOSE

Most studies of international franchising have been conducted in the 1990s and to date there is generally a scarcity of empirical and conceptual research on the topic (Ackerman, Bush and Justis 1994; Fladmoe-Lindquist 1996; Shane 1996b; Fladmoe-Lindquist and Jacque 1995; Huszagh et al. 1992). Fladmoe-Lindquist (1996) wrote that international franchising research has been limited to problems, motivating factors, constraining factors, and managerial attitudes. The purpose of this study is to extend the existing literature of international franchising by developing a model which incorporates elements from both resource-based and agency theories. These theories were previously used in the domestic context and only recently in the international franchising environment. To achieve its purpose this study reviews literature from Marketing, Economics, International Business, Management, Finance, Law, popular business magazines, case studies, franchising books, governmental organizations, the International Franchising Association, and consulting firms, in particular Arthur Andersen.

IMPORTANCE OF THE STUDY

International franchising research explanations divide into organizational and environmental causal factors. Environmental explanations of international franchising include the life cycle theory, domestic market saturation hypothesis, and country factors influencing US international franchising expansion. These explanations of international franchising are incomplete because they cannot explain why some firms within the same industry internationalize while others do not (Shane 1996b). Shane (1996b, p. 75) claimed that "a complete explanation of the adoption of international expansion strategy must consider firm elements." His study examined why some US franchisors decide to explore global markets using agency theory. Shane's (1996b) examination of franchising is innovative because (1) he identified firm factors contributing to the decision to internationalize, (2) he framed the decision of franchisors to internationalize in the agency theory perspective, and (3) his model exhibited strong explanatory power. It is the purpose of this study to extend Shane's theory by including the resource-based theory in the explanation of why US franchisors internationalize.

The study is different from Shane's (1996b) study in several ways. First, it incorporates resource-based theory and agency theory into an explanation of the internationalization of US franchisors. Studies of domestic franchising increased their explanatory ability when both perspectives were incorporated (Combs and Castrogiovanni 1994; Carney and Gedajlovic 1991). Carney and Gedajlovic (1991) stated that a full explanation of franchising necessitates both the agency and resource-based perspectives. Secondly, this study examines international franchising over time: 1990–1997. Using 1994 as the year of analysis, Shane's (1996b) study used a cross-sectional approach to testing his theory. A pooled time-series approach may be more appropriate because the decision to internationalize is dynamic in nature and because it enlarges the sample size for each industry. Finally, Shane's (1996b) study attempted to generalize across all industries, assuming the causal connections are the same. This study investigates the internationalization of three industrial sectors separately because (1) the determinants of international franchising can be different from one industry to another, and (2) some industries have a greater rate of internationalization.

The results of this study may be useful to academics and practitioners alike. On the theoretical front, this study is path breaking because (1) it develops a theoretical model which includes two powerful theories of domestic franchising, (2) it tests this model empirically improving on the methodological problems of past research, (3) it helps resolve the debate of whether resource-based theories provide a compelling explanation for franchising, and (4) it provides insight into the internationalization of the US service sector. On the practical side, this study can potentially be used by franchisors or franchisees. Using the logistic regression coefficients derived in this study franchisors or prospective franchisees will be able to predict the probability that the franchisor will internationalize.

RESEARCH DESIGN

Two competing paradigms, resource based and agency theories, are integrated and reviewed to arrive at an organizational explanation of international franchising. Using the paradigms of resource-based and agency theory, this study develops research questions that focus on the organizational characteristics of the firm, helping to explain why some franchising companies within the same industry internationalize. These general questions are then framed into formal hypotheses that are tested against data in three industries provided by *Entrepreneur* magazine in the period 1990–1997.

Research Questions

To facilitate understanding of international franchising, the following research questions are developed:
1) What firm characteristics of the franchisor are associated with international franchising expansion (significance); and
2) How do these characteristics affect the desire of the franchisors to expand internationally (directionality).

Research Hypotheses

The following research hypotheses were developed:

Resource-based Theory

H1: The bigger the franchisor, the more likely it is to seek international franchisees.
H2: The older the franchisor, the more likely it is to seek international franchisees.
H3: The higher the rate of growth of the franchising system, the more likely it is to seek international franchisees.

Agency Theory

H4: The higher the price bonding in the pricing structure, the more likely the franchisor is to seek international franchisees.

H5: The greater the geographical dispersion of franchisees in the franchisor's system, the more likely the franchisor is to seek international franchisees.

SCOPE OF THE STUDY

This study focuses on the internationalization of US franchisors. United States franchising data are used because of data availability and the fact that the United States is the world's largest source of international franchising. The study is further limited to three industrial sectors: (1) retailing, (2) professional business services, and (3) hotels and motels. The retail sector includes a variety of consumer goods' stores.[1] The professional business service sector consists of accounting and tax services, advertising and promotional systems, business brokerages, and consulting services. The hotels and motels category includes hotels at the economy, midrange, and luxury levels. The scope of the analysis allows for cross-industrial comparisons.

METHODOLOGY

Franchising Data

In 1987 the US Office of Management and Budget ceased funding for the collection of international franchising data by the US Department of Commerce because "it did not have direct implications to federal policy making" (Committee on Small Business 1990, p. 14). To fill the gap in data collection a number of private sources attempted to collect franchising data. The most notable is *Entrepreneur Magazine*. *Entrepreneur Magazine* has published a "Franchise 500" survey in

---

1. The retail sector includes apparel and accessories, appliances, furniture, art products, bookstores, CDs/Tape stores, gifts and flowers, greeting card distribution, hardware, newsstands, party stores, pharmacies, stationery stores, videocassette rentals, video game stores, water sales, discount/variety stores, and miscellaneous retail businesses.

January of every year since 1970. This data set includes key firm characteristics of over 1000 franchisors. These characteristics include (1) the nature of the business, (2) the year the business began, (3) the year franchising began, (4) where the franchisor is seeking franchisees, (5) the number of franchisee and company owned outlets, (6) the franchising fee, (7) the start-up costs, (8) the royalties, (9) the type of financing that is available, and (10) franchise 500 ranking.

This data set was used in both domestic franchising (Combs and Castrogiovanni 1994; Martin and Justis 1993) and international franchising (Shane 1996b) studies. Although the inclusion of franchisors in the survey is voluntary, several researchers suggested that no serious biases exist (Combs and Castrogiovanni 1994). Furthermore, the magazine itself validates over 80 percent of the data through the Uniform Franchise Offering Circular, a prospectus containing key information required by US regulations.

Data Analysis

The independent and control variables are analyzed through logistic regression. This method is useful when researchers want to establish a causal relationship between a nonmetric dependent variable and multiple independent variables (Hair et al. 1992). Using data from *Entrepreneur*, Shane (1996b) used logistic regression to explain the internationalization of US franchisors. His study however modeled the dynamic phenomenon of franchising using cross-sectional data and focused entirely on agency theory. This study extends Shane's (1996b) study by incorporating variables from resource based theory and examining international franchising over-time. Following Shane's (1996b) methodology, this study uses logistic regression to analyze the variables. Unlike his methodology, however, this study examines time-series instead of cross-sectional data and divides the analysis by industry level rather than viewing all franchising as one aggregate unit.

ORGANIZATION OF THIS STUDY

This study is divided into six chapters. This chapter (chapter I) includes an introduction to the study, a statement of purpose, research design, and an overview of the organization of the study. Chapter II provides the literature review. This includes the nature and scope of international franchising and a review of environmental and organizational variables of international franchising. A theoretical model which integrates the agency and resource based theories of international franchising is developed in chapter III.

Chapter IV explains the research design and the methodology. Emphasis will be given to the rational for the choice of logistic regression analysis and the interpretation of logistic regression coefficients. Chapter IV shows how key organizational factors explain the variations in the desire of the United States franchisors to internationalize. The link between the research questions and testable hypotheses is made in this chapter.

Chapter V is the heart of the study as it provides the results of the analysis. The full model is delineated and explained for each industry. These explanations include descriptive statistics, tests of the model, significance of the variables, and the importance of the various factors influencing international franchising. Each of the three industries is investigated individually.

Chapter VI includes a discussion of the results. A discussion of each hypothesis is provided, synthesizing the results obtained in chapter V. This is followed by a conclusion, implications to practitioners, and the possibility for future research.

CHAPTER II

Literature of International Franchising

INTRODUCTION

The beginning of franchising has been traced back to King John of England in the Middle Ages granting franchises to tax collectors (Hoffman and Preble 1991), and to German brewers in the eighteenth century granting exclusive rights to sell particular brands of beer (Hackett 1976). But franchising did not experience real growth until it reached the US in the mid 1800s. Singer Sewing Machine, followed by the soft drink and automobile industries, and later by petroleum producers, adopted the system of what is currently known as first-generation franchising, or product/trade-name franchising (Hackett 1976). "Product/trade-name franchising is a distribution system in which suppliers make contracts with dealers to buy or sell products or product lines" (Falbe and Dandridge 1992, p. 43). Between 1972 and 1988 the number of product/trade-name franchisors declined by roughly one half. Product/trade-name franchising accounted for less than 30 percent of all franchise business in 1990 (Committee on Small Business 1990).

In the 1950s a second generation of franchising, called business format franchising, fueled the franchising frenzy (Hoffman and Preble 1991). The difference between product/trade-name franchising and business format franchising is that the latter offers a method of operation, or business system, which includes a strategic plan for growth and ongoing guidance (Falbe and Dandridge 1992). Unlike product/trade-name franchising, the number of business format outlets has increased almost tenfold between 1972 to 1988 (Kostecka 1988), with international expansion reaching a growth rate of 17 percent per year (Shane 1996b). By the year 2000 most US franchisors are expected to have international operations (Hoffman and Preble 1993). Business format franchising is the basis for most successful ventures in global franchising and market entry analysis usually focuses on this form of franchising (Burton and Cross 1995). For these reasons, this paper concentrates on business format franchising[2]

INTERNATIONAL FRANCHISING DEFINITIONS

Burton and Cross (1995, p. 36) defined international franchising as "a foreign market entry mode that involves a relationship between the entrant (the franchisor) and a host country entity, in which the former transfers, under contract, a business package (or format), which it has developed and owns, to the latter." This host country entity can be either a domestic franchisee, a foreign franchisee, a master franchisor, or an entity which is partly owned by the franchisor itself.

International franchising has been typically treated as a type of licensing (Ackerman et al. 1994; Dahringer and Muhlbacher 1991; Root 1987; Boddewyn et al. 1986). Root (1987, p. 109) proposed that "franchising is a form of licensing in which a company (franchisor) licenses a business system as well as other property rights to an independent company or person (franchisee)." Root (1987, p. 85) defined licensing as "a variety of contractual arrangements whereby domestic companies (licensors) made available their intangible assets (patents, trade secrets, know-how, trade marks, and company name) to foreign companies (licensees) in return for royalties and/or other forms of payment."

Unlike licensing, franchising may provide tangible as well as intangible assets. The franchisor often provides an input into the production of the franchisee's product or service. Furthermore, a study of US international franchisors by Arthur Andersen (1996) found that the average investment in international franchising was about $680,000. Therefore, the traditional view of international franchising as licensing

---

2.   For purpose of brevity, from here on the word franchising will refer to business format franchising.

may be erroneously rooted in the assumption that international franchising is a non-equity and non-direct mode of entry (Burton and Cross 1995). Burton and Cross (1995) proposed that as the percentage ownership of international franchising approaches 100 percent, it resembles foreign direct investment more than licensing.

Ackerman et al. (1994) equated international franchising to exporting because both are means of entering global markets with little investment and limited risk. The experience of many franchisors reveals that entering a foreign market involves at least some investment by the international franchisor (Love 1995; Arthur Andersen 1996). Furthermore, unlike exporting, international franchising requires close attention to tracking down equipment, securing local raw materials that meet the franchisor's quality specifications, and protecting trade marks and trade secrets (Steinberg 1992). Therefore, equating international franchising to exporting may be erroneous.

Finally, international franchising is often distinct from direct investment. Boddewyn et al. (1986) stated that franchising in its purest form does not involve equity investment by the franchisor. Therefore, it cannot be considered a form of foreign direct investment. It was later shown that different modes of international franchising require different levels of financial exposure. Aydin and Kacker (1990) proposed that international franchising has several characteristics distinguishing it from other forms of international business such as foreign direct investment. These are broken down into three categories: (1) firm characteristics, (2) source country, and (3) recipient country. From the franchising firm's perspective, the standardized nature of franchising necessitates a high degree of cooperation and control by the franchisor. This may be difficult in a multicultural context. Franchising operations are more immune to foreign exchange risk because most inputs are provided locally (Aydin and Kacker 1990). The franchisor is also less affected by failure risk because ownership is often assumed by the franchisee. From the source-country perspective, unlike foreign direct investment, international franchising is not associated with home-country job loss because most international franchising operations are services unsuitable for exporting. Finally, from the host-country perspective, the balance of payments is not as severely affected as in the case of foreign direct investment. This is because of minimal import content, low capital outflow, and little repatriation of profits because ownership is often local (Aydin and Kacker 1990).

Because of the unique nature of international franchising, Burton and Cross (1995) claimed that, theoretically speaking, the international franchising mode of entry should be treated as a separate construct because (1) characteristics of the business stay the same regardless of who is the owner and (2) ownership can be transformed with relative ease, even after operations have been established, without any noticeable difference. Shane (1996b, p. 86) concluded that "the use of franchise contracts appears to be an important long-term strategic choice in its own right for international service firms, rather than a temporary arrangement on the journey to full corporate ownership of foreign operations."

The research on international franchising falls into two categories: (1) environmental explanations, and (2) organizational explanations. Economic, demographic, distance, and political factors are responsible for the proliferation of international franchising according to the first research stream. The modes of entry in international franchising research focused on two aspects: (1) the choice between company ownership and franchising, and (2) the choice between various franchising modes of entry. Finally, organizational explanations focused on company capabilities and characteristics. These include the franchising resource-based and agency theories. Shane (1996b) stated that an explanation of international franchising must consider firm variables because environmental variables are incapable of explaining why some firms within the same industry internationalize.

THEORIES OF INTERNATIONAL FRANCHISING

Explanations of international franchising divide into environmental (external) and organizational (internal) factors. Figure 2.1 shows a comprehensive paradigm of international franchising using both environmental and organizational factors.

Figure 2.1: A Paradigms of International Franchising

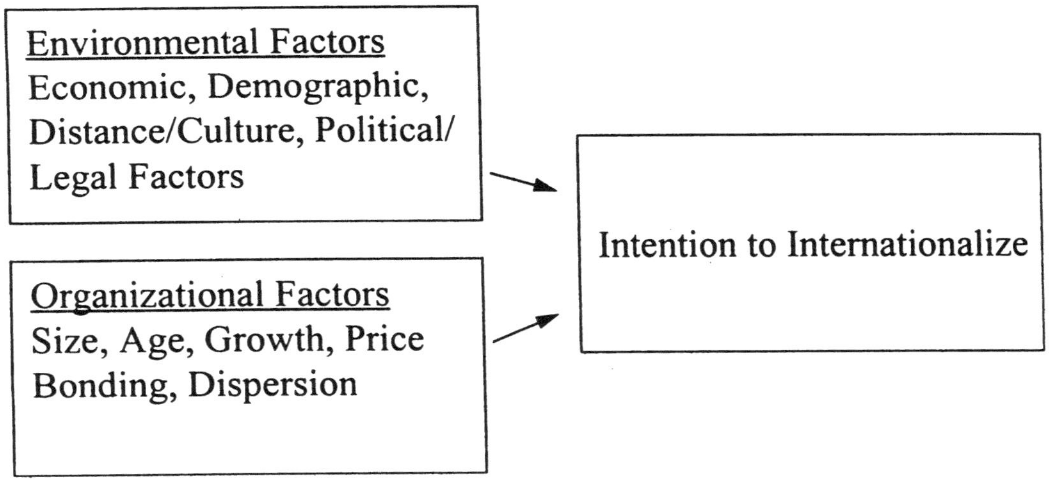

The focus of this study is on organizational factors since environmental factors can not explain why some franchisors within ̄ industry internationalize. However, in the interest of a balanced presentation, the remainder of this chapter examines both the environmental and organizational explanations of international franchising. Chapter III develops the hypotheses associated with organizational factors of international franchising for subsequent testing.

Environmental Factors of International Franchising

In the context of environmental explanations for the globalization of the US franchising system, international franchising researchers, practitioners, and consulting firms have begun to chart out the country characteristics that are important to international franchisors. International franchising surveys and econometric studies are analyzed to extract the key host-country variables affecting the number of US international franchising companies. These variables fall into four categories: (1) economic, (2) demographic, (3) distance, and (4) political factors (See table 2.1). Alon and McKee (1999) integrated these four factors to develop a normative macro-environmental model of international franchising.

Table 2.1: Environmental Factors of International Franchising

Factor	Mentioned by
Economic	Kostecka (1988); Hackett (1976)
Income/GDP	Aydin and Kacker (1990); Yavas and Vardiabasis (1987); Arthur Andersen (1996) Trankiem (1979); Welch (1989)
Per capita income	Welch (1989); Kostecka (1988)
Income growth	Yavas and Vardiabasis (1987); Arthur Andersen (1996)
Urbanization	Yavas and Vardiabasis (1987); Arthur Andersen (1996); Norton (1988)
Retail/service sector	Welch (1989); Arthur Andersen (1996)
Tourism	Kostecka (1988); Norton (1988)
Demographic	
Middle class	Arthur Andersen (1996)
Population growth	Arthur Andersen (1996)
Education	Arthur Andersen (1996)
Female labor participation	Yavas and Vardiabasis (1987); Arthur Andersen (1996);
Distance/culture	
Physical distance	Welch (1989); Kostecka (1988); Huszagh et al. (1992); Arthur Andersen (1996); Fladmoe-Lindquist (1996); Brickley and Dark (1987)
Cultural distance	Welch (1989); Arthur Andersen (1996); Fladmoe-Lindquist (1996)
Use of English	Kostecka (1988); Arthur Andersen (1996)
Political/Legal	
Political risk	Burton and Cross (1995); Alon (1996)
gov't control	Kostecka (1988)
gov't restrictions	Walker and Etzel (1973)
political stability	Arthur Andersen (1996)

The Economic Dimension

Market potential was the most frequently mentioned determinant for the expansion of US international franchising into foreign markets (Trankiem 1979; Kostecka 1988; Hackett 1976; Aydin and Kacker

1990; Yavas and Vardiabasis 1987; Arthur Andersen 1996; Welch 1989). Yavas and Vardiabasis (1987) confirmed the hypothesis that a positive relationship exists between market size and the number of units of US fast-food franchises in the Pacific Basin. A number of researchers specified other proxies of market potential. Yavas and Vardiabasis (1987) and Arthur Andersen (1996) suggested that income growth was an important variable for US international franchising expansion. Yavas and Vardiabasis (1987) tested the income-growth hypothesis and found no significant relationship between income growth and the number of units of US fast-food franchising.

Urbanization was another economic factor cited in the literature. A survey study of US international franchisors by Arthur Andersen (1996) revealed that urbanization is the fifth most important variable in determining whether a foreign country is likely to be receptive to the US franchising system. Using population density as a proxy for the level of urbanization, Yavas and Vardiabasis (1987) tested the hypothesis that there is a positive association between a host country's population density and the number of US franchises and found no significant relationship.

Welch (1989) proposed that US international franchising to English speaking developed countries was partly related to these countries' highly developed retail and service sectors. Indeed, much US international franchising to these countries was in hotels and motels, restaurants, retailing, and rental services (Justis and Judd 1989), all part of the retail and service sectors in the economy. Kostecka (1988) proposed that these industries may be related to the level of tourism in the country. Norton (1988) found that the propensity to franchise is related to travel intensity.

The Demographic Dimension

Several demographic variables were mentioned in the literature. Arthur Andersen (1996) discovered the existence of a substantial middle class as the most important factor in determining whether a host country will be suitable to the US franchising system. Other population characteristics have been mentioned explicitly and implicitly. Arthur Andersen (1996) reported that more than 60 percent of the responding franchisors considered population growth an important determinant for choosing a host country. Other researchers were more subtle. Welch

(1989) and Kostecka (1988) implicitly considered population when they discussed the importance of a high per capita income. Several researchers identified labor characteristics. The level of education was mentioned to be important or most important by almost 60 percent of all respondents (Arthur Andersen 1996). Yavas and Vardiabasis (1987) investigated the relationship between female labor participation and the expansion of US fast-food franchising. They found a significant relationship between these two constructs. On the other hand, the Arthur Andersen (1996) survey indicated that the ratio of working women was considered to be one of the least important variables in determining whether a foreign country is likely to be receptive to the US franchising system.

The Distance Dimension

Physical distance was one of the most mentioned factors in US international franchising expansion (Welch 1989; Kostecka 1988; Huszagh et al. 1992; Arthur Andersen 1996). Fladmoe-Lindquist (1996) posed the problem of physical distance from the standpoint of administrative efficiency theory. Physical distance makes it difficult and expensive to receive complete and timely information about a foreign operation. Communications technology is not perfectly standardized across and among countries because of software, hardware, connectivity, and regulations regarding transmission (Fladmoe-Lindquist 1996).

The nature of franchising requires contracting between the franchisee and franchisor. In the domestic environment contracting can be standardized, but in a global environment contracts vary greatly. Fee structures, cooperative advertisement, and support functions are modified for different countries because of differences in size of franchisees, host-country restrictions, indigenous practices, and entrepreneurial behavior.

Cultural distance, including the use of English, is an important determinant of the success of a US international franchisor (Welch 1989; Arthur Andersen 1996; Aydin and Kacker 1990). Culture affects contract negotiation, operations, personnel, hiring, and franchising format (Fladmoe-Lindquist 1996; Justis and Judd 1989). "The transferability of the [franchising] system becomes a function of cultural distance between the foreign and domestic cultures. The very strength of a franchising format, its standardization, makes its successful replication in foreign markets difficult" (Fladmoe-Lindquist 1996, p. 425). Huszagh et al. (1992) proposed that the industries that reflect US lifestyles are more likely to succeed overseas. They pointed to the internationalization of restaurant franchises in the 1970s to support their position.

The Political Dimension

Numerous "how-to" articles and books describe the importance of traditional political-risk variables in international franchising. These variables include: (1) governmental regulations and red tape (Falbe and Dandridge 1992; Kostecka 1988; Justis and Judd 1989), (2) political stability (Falbe and Dandridge 1992; Justis and Judd 1989), (3) monetary/exchange controls (Committee on Small business; Justis and Judd 1989), (4) proliferation of bribery (Justis and Judd 1989), (5) import restrictions (Committee on Small Business 1991; Justis and Judd 1989; Falbe and Dandridge 1992), and (6) ownership restrictions (Justis and Judd 1989; Falbe and Dandridge 1992). Furthermore, US franchisors reported host-government regulations and red tape, import restrictions, and monetary uncertainties as the three highest ranking problems encountered in international markets (Hackett 1976). The importance of many political-risk variables to international franchisors signifies that political risk may play an important role in international franchising and, thus, challenges the traditional view of franchising.

Aydin and Kacker (1990) and Hoffman and Preble (1991) proposed that international franchising is lower in political risk than foreign direct investment because (1) local franchisees are assumed to incur the investment and, therefore, the political risk, and (2) foreign exchange risk is lower because the import-export content of local operations is minimal. There are several weaknesses with their arguments. First, Burton and Cross (1995, p. 45) wrote that "firms employing franchising contracts in their internationalization process can, and frequently do, invest significant amounts of equity in host country franchise subsystems." Therefore, the assumption of low investment by the international franchisor may be erroneous. Their second argument has two weaknesses. First, many franchisors require their franchisees to purchase their operating supplies from them (Fladmoe-Lindquist 1996), therefore increasing the import-export ratio and their exposure to exchange risk. Hunt and Nevin (1975) wrote that 70 percent of surveyed franchisees in the US were required to purchase a median of 50 percent of their operating supplies. Second, royalties may be adversely influenced by foreign-exchange fluctuations caused by political risk. Furthermore, Fladmoe-Lindquist (1996) wrote that a host country policy evaluation and exchange rate management are two key host-country risk management skills a global franchisor must possess. Therefore, political risk is an important variable to the international franchisor.

Perhaps the confusion regarding the assumption that international franchising has minimal political risk exposure is a result of the perceived nature of international franchising. As mentioned earlier, early researchers equated franchising to licensing, probably because of its association with first-generation franchising. Licensing involves the transfer of a trademark with minimal investment (Boddewyn et al. 1986). Indeed, licensing involves less political risk than FDI. This is because (1) host governments prefer it as a means of transferring technology (Root 1987; Eiteman et al. 1991), (2) this mode of entry is immune to expropriation (Root 1987), and (3) local constituents may have more political leverage, as in the case of India. Unlike licensing, a survey by the US Department of Commerce found that some foreign governments dislike the use of franchising because of the public association of franchising with pyramid marketing schemes (Kostecka 1973).

Organizational Factors of International Franchising

Organizational factors of international franchising include (1) franchising life cycle, (2) domestic market saturation, (3) resource-based, and (4) agency theories. The first two theories can apply both at the industry and the firm levels.

Franchise Life Cycle Theory

A seminal article by Welch (1989) described US international franchising development in a similar fashion in which Vernon (1966) explicated the international product life cycle concept. Welch (1989) asserted that initial international franchising expansion was to Canada because of physical proximity and cultural similarity. Australia, the UK, and Japan were early recipients of US international franchising because of high per capita income, highly developed retail and service sectors, and, in the case of Australia and the UK, cultural similarity.

Much of the expansion to Japan was in the form of master franchising. The master has major responsibilities in selling franchises, qualifying franchisees, collecting franchise and royalty fees, product modifications, and in training and supporting activities (Justis and Judd 1986). Therefore, cultural proximity was not as important a variable in Japan which has had a very high per capita GDP and a substantial service sector. The very nature of franchising which offers standard formulae made it prone to imitation. Early recipients of US international franchising emulated US systems in their own country. Later, they expanded back into the US because the US possesses high per capita income and highly developed retail and service sectors.

In recent years there have been signs that foreign-based franchisors are entering the US (Zeidman 1992). These countries include mostly developed countries, or first stage countries, such as Australia (Welch 1989). The second stage countries to which US international franchisors entered are countries of greater diversity of culture, income, and political systems. With these countries, however, US franchisors limited their risk and involvement by contracting with local agents through either joint ventures or master agreements. Welch (1989) predicted that franchising systems from developing nations will eventually penetrate the US and other developed nations as these nations imitate the newly acquired marketing systems. According to Welch (1989), therefore, the country variables that initially influenced US international franchising expansion were the economic level of development, the size of the service sector, and cultural proximity. This was followed by an expansion into developing and less developed countries. Over time, these countries emulated American franchising systems and exported their own franchising versions back into the United States.

Domestic Market Saturation

The domestic market saturation explanation of international franchising is compatible with the franchise life cycle theory. A firm's growth within a geographical area is finite because franchisees are allotted geographical exclusivity and prime locations are scarce. Saturation in the domestic market pushed franchisors to internationalize in an effort to look for viable markets for their products and services. Aydin and Kacker (1990), Hackett (1976), and Yavas and Vardiabasis (1987) proposed that the internationalization of franchising systems may be a natural response to domestic market saturation. According to this theory, when franchising firms exhaust the domestic market, they look abroad for growth. Therefore, the greater the number of outlets a firm has, the more likely it is to internationalize.

Resource-Based Theories

Resource-based theories explain the internationalization of franchising systems as a function of the amount of the firm's resources. Resources include human and nonhuman capital such as money, lines of credit, managers, workers, and connections abroad. Resources in empirical investigations have been measured by the size, age and growth of the firm. The assumption is that the bigger, older and faster-growing the company, the more likely it is to posses the resources needed for internationalization. Internationalization, therefore, is hypothesized to be positively related to the age, size, and growth rate of the franchising firm.

Agency Theories

Agency theories in franchising have examined the relationship between the franchisor and the franchisee. In the international context, franchisors are more difficult to monitor and control because of geographical distance and communication problems. Therefore, firms seek to minimize their exposure by developing better controlling and monitoring systems. The literature of international franchising suggested that pricing the franchises such that the majority of the payment will be made up-front reduces the payment risk as well as ensuring that franchisees will follow the franchisor's protocols. Second, operating across a wide geographic area can increase the monitoring capabilities of the firm. Therefore, US firms that operate in multiple states are more likely to internationalize than ones that are local players.

CONCLUSION

This chapter shows that the proper conceptual framework for international franchising should not follow that of licensing, foreign direct investment, or exporting. This is because international franchising is a unique method of entry that is based on complex contractual arrangements that bond the franchisor and the franchisee. This study is based on resource-based and agency theories of franchising which have been used to explain the internationalization of franchising systems (Fladmoe-Lindquist 1996; Shane 1996b; Fladmoe-Lindquist and Jacque 1995).

The use of both resource-based and agency approaches in the international franchising literature is a departure from their use in the domestic context. These theories use the base-line approach of agency and resource-based explanations, but the emphasis is different. In the domestic context, agency and resource-based theories were used to explain why some companies used franchising while others expanded through company owned outlets, while in the international context the focus was on the decision to internationalize. Because most franchisors increasingly chose third-party ownership, such as master franchising, as a means of expansion into global markets over company ownership (Hackett 1976; Kostecka 1988; Arthur Andersen 1996), a salient question in international franchising is, therefore, whether to franchise in international markets or stay as a domestic player. The next chapter develops a model for the internationalization of US franchising systems using resource-based and agency theories.

CHAPTER III
The Model

INTRODUCTION TO MODEL DEVELOPMENT

This chapter provides the theoretical framework for investigating the organizational factors of internationalization. While environmental factors can explain why some countries have higher shares of US international franchising, or why a particular method of entry was chosen in a particular country, they cannot adequately explain why some firms within the same industry internationalize while others do not. Environmental explanations of international franchising are incomplete because they cannot explain why some companies franchise internationally while others do not (Shane 1996b).

A need exists to identify the characteristics of franchising firms that are associated with international expansion. Organizational explanations of international franchising have focused on firm characteristics and capabilities associated with international franchising. In this chapter, resource-based and agency theories are used to develop a model which uses firm-level variables to explain the internationalization of US franchising firms within industries. Both agency (Shane 1996b) and resource-based (Fladmoe-Lindquist 1996) theories were used to explain the internationalization of the US franchising system.

While the agency theory has been tested and the initial empirical results of the theory are encouraging, resource-based explanations for international franchising have hardly been tested. Fladmoe-Lindquist (1996) and Huszagh et al. (1992) developed a rationale for using the resources of the firm to explain its propensity to internationalize.

Huszagh et al. (1992, p. 7) wrote "franchising by its very nature requires significant amounts of externally-sourced capital which is then dispersed across many, geographically separated 'production centres'. Thus, capital requirements and geographic separation raise the need for continuous access to capital, on the one hand, and pose particular monitoring problems for the franchisor, on the other." Franchisors who wish to internationalize need to have sufficient resources (Fladmoe-Lindquist 1996) and need to protect themselves against shirking and opportunistic behavior by the franchisee (Shane 1996b).

Fladmoe-Lindquist (1996) focused on the company characteristics associated with international franchising using both agency and resource-based theories. He developed a conceptual explanation for international franchising. Shane (1996b) used agency theory to develop an empirical model explaining the propensity of franchisors to internationalize. It is the purpose of this study to extend their work by developing a model that incorporates elements of both resource-based and agency theories to explain the internationalization of the United States franchising industry. This study tests the resource-based explanations for international franchising and checks the conclusions derived from Shane's study (1996b).

THE MODEL

Resource-Based Theory

The resource-based theory of domestic franchising postulates that companies franchise in order to obtain needed resources for domestic expansion. For international expansion, the need for resources is even more pronounced because of environmental differences and cultural dissimilarities. It is unlikely and extremely risky for a franchisor to internationalize prematurely. Mendelsohn (1994, p. 62) wrote: "even if the franchise business can command a substantial initial fee, it will be incurring expenses long before it receives anything."

Fladmoe-Lindquist (1996) showed that franchisors must possess key resources before being able to internationalize successfully. Resources that were mentioned in the franchising literature include (1) capital requirements (Hunt 1973), (2) human capital (Norton 1988), (3) managerial talent (Oxenfeldt and Kelly 1969; Combs and Castrogiovanni 1994), (4) local knowledge (Combs and Castrogiovanni 1994), and (5) distance management, cultural adaptability, and host country risk management skills (Fladmoe-Lindquist 1996). The franchising system acquires these resources over time as it gains experience in the domestic market. Huszagh et al. (1992) wrote that international franchisors have greater cumulative experience, scale economies, product differentiation, capital requirements and benefits of headquarters. This allows them to erect entry barriers against new firms and to compete successfully overseas.

As the firm grows by developing additional franchised outlets, it develops the resources which allow it to acquire the firm characteristics that are needed for international expansion. As the number of franchised outlets increase, so do the franchise fees, royalties, and economies of scale. Economies of scale in purchasing, promotion, R&D, monitoring, and quality programs can facilitate cost reductions that would allow a franchisor to compete effectively in international markets. The more units that the franchising system has, the more efficient are the monitoring and performance measuring capabilities. This is because the mere volume of these comparisons have the potential to generate more educated routines for identifying shirking (Huszagh et al. 1992). Monitoring capabilities reduce the costs of opportunism by the franchisee, allowing international expansion through franchising (Shane 1996b; Fladmoe-Lindquist 1996).

The size of the franchising firm also influences its market power and credibility. "It would be easier to raise a comparable amount of capital for a franchised unit of a large franchise than a small one" (Huszagh et al. 1992, p. 16). Bigger firms with more outlets are more well-known and have more leverage in raising capital both domestically and internationally. Domestic capital can be used to help in the expansion of international franchisees when foreign capital market are inadequate.

There is also a greater probability that larger franchising firms have saturated the domestic market and are looking for growth through international expansion (Shane 1996b). The more outlets the franchise system has, the more likely it is to saturate the market and look for expansion overseas. An example of a firm that aggressively seeks expansion through international franchising partly because it has saturated the domestic market is McDonald's.

Past research indicates that bigger franchising firms have a higher preponderance for having units outside the United States (Hackett 1976; Walker and Etzel 1973). Aydin and Kacker (1990) showed that smaller franchising systems are less likely to seek international franchisees than bigger ones. Huszagh et al. (1992) found a significant positive association between the number of units and the decision to internationalize in both 1967 and 1988. However, they expected that technology, in particular in telecommunications, would mitigate the influence of scale on the internationalization of franchising systems in 1988. This was not the case. A recent survey by Arthur Andersen (1996) revealed that franchisors with over 86 units were more likely to belong to the International Franchise Association and have franchises operating outside the United States. Eroglu (1992p. 24) wrote that "since larger franchise systems have more resources to allocate, and a higher capacity to absorb failure, they are expected to influence management's risk perception inversely such that the larger the system size, the less the possible impact of cost and, therefore, the lower the overall perceived risk associated with international expansion." Therefore,

H1: The bigger the franchisor, the more likely it is to seek international franchisees.

It is likely that the older the franchising firm, the more resources it will have. This is because it will have more experience borne out of operating domestically. Experience should make an older firm more cost-efficient, and therefore more competitive in domestic and international markets. In franchising, experience in site selection, store layout, procurement and operation policies can facilitate cost reductions based on improved know-how (Huszagh et al. 1992). Therefore, experience and know-how would allow an older franchising firm to successfully transfer the operating system of a franchise to a foreign market with more ease than a younger franchisor.

Past research (Hackett 1976; Walker and Etzel 1973) as well as recent research (Arthur Andersen 1996; Huszagh et al. 1992) on franchising showed that older franchisors are more inclined to have international franchisees. When franchisors without international franchises were asked why their company does not have franchises outside the United States, the number one reason given in 1995 was that the company was too young (Arthur Andersen 1996). Eroglu

(1992) proposed that the older and more experienced a franchisor, the lower the amount of perceived risk associated with internationalization, and the more likely the franchisor will seek international franchisees. Huszagh et al. (1992) showed that the age of the franchising system was positively related to its decision to internationalize in both 1967 and 1988. "These findings imply that experience is still a powerful tool for dealing with the physical and cultural distance inherent in franchising overseas. The inability of technology to substitute for experience appears to be borne out by these results" (Huszagh et al. 1992, p. 14). Therefore,

H2: The older the franchisor, the more likely it is to seek international franchisees.

The greater the rate of growth in the number of outlets, the more resources the franchising firm has, and the more likely it will internationalize. Shane (1996b) pointed out that the higher the growth of the franchisor, the more successful it is and, therefore, the more resources it may have to devote to its globalization efforts. "One could argue that more successful firms should be more interested in overseas expansion because their greater resource slack and greater ability to obtain resources from capital markets should make them better able than less successful firms to absorb the risks and costs of such expansion" (Shane 1996b, p. 81). The growth rate also indicates that the business system developed by the franchisor is attractive to potential franchisees. The fast growth of a franchising system is an indication that the business is successful and is a selling point for the franchisor who wants to lure in domestic and international investors. Therefore,

H3: The higher the rate of growth of the franchising system, the more likely it is to seek international franchisees.

Agency Theory

The focus of agency theory is to minimize agency costs, especially the ones associated with shirking and monitoring costs. Based on these premises, Shane (1996b) developed a model that explains the internationalization of the US franchising system as a function of bonding and learned monitoring capabilities. Shane (1996b) claimed that franchisee opportunism can be reduced through ex-ante bonding mechanisms, or a pricing structure that requires high initial investment relative to royalties. The franchising firm controls the ratio between the initial payment and the ongoing payments. In this fashion it controls the bonding. The higher the level of bonding, the less the probability that a franchisee will act opportunistically. This is because (1) the franchisee fee accounts for one-half of the total investment of the franchisee, (2) the franchisee invests a major portion of his/her wealth in the business, (3) the standard franchising agreement allows franchisors to revoke the contract without the return of the fee if the franchisee does not obey a strict format, and (4) the cost of termination increases the higher the initial fee relative to the ongoing fees. "As the threat of opportunism is greater in international franchising than domestic franchising, one would expect to find higher franchise fees relative to royalty and advertising rates among companies that intend to expand overseas" (Shane 1996b, p. 77). Shane measured the ex-ante bond as a ratio between the initial fee and the ongoing fees and found support for the hypothesis that ex-ante bonding increases the likelihood of internationalization of the franchise system.

International franchising operations require that the franchisor manage a remote location. Because remote locations have higher monitoring costs (Combs and Castrogiovanni 1994; Brickley and Dark 1987; Norton 1988), franchisors can price their business system such that the franchisee bears the risk. This is done by increasing the initial investment relative to the ongoing payments, or decreasing the royalties relative to the franchise fee. In this situation the franchisor is in a position to gain the franchise fee regardless of whether the business entity succeeds or fails. The advantage of using this price bonding variable is that this ratio is controlled by the franchisor.

Combs and Castrogiovanni (1994, p. 42) defined royalties as the "proportion of the present value of intangible resources that cannot be incorporated into the up-front fee due to the unpredictability of unit sales." Because international sales of US franchising systems are more unpredictable overseas than domestically, international franchisors would rather receive more of the money up-front, rather than over time in the form of royalties. A survey by Arthur Andersen (1996) showed that the initial franchise fees of international units tend to be the same or higher, while the ongoing payments tend to be the same or lower. This result is consistent with Shane's (1996) finding on the effect of price bonding. Therefore,

H4: The greater the price bonding, the more likely the franchisor is to seek international franchisees.

A second method of minimizing opportunism is through the development of monitoring capabilities. Monitoring capabilities are critical to the success of the international franchisor (Fladmoe-Lindquist 1996). Shane (1996b) found support for the hypothesis that better monitoring skills increase the propensity of franchisors to internationalize. He measured monitoring skills as a multiplicative composite index consisting of the number of franchised units, the percentage of franchised outlets, and the age of the franchise system. There is no theoretical reason why a multiplicative measure was used. Furthermore, the variables are likely to be correlated, obfuscating the regression coefficient results. For this reason, this study uses the measure of geographical dispersion for monitoring capabilities.

According to agency theory, franchisors with dispersed units require greater monitoring capabilities (Fladmoe-Lindquist 1996). Franchisors with many franchisees in heterogeneous locations across the United States are better poised to take advantage of economies of scale in promotion and monitoring because such locations incorporate differing levels of return and risk (Huszagh et al. 1992). Therefore, franchisors which are national in scope are more likely to internationalize because they have the monitoring capabilities in their domestic operations. The foreign subsidiary becomes an extension to the domestic operation. This is especially true for franchisors which first seek international expansion in Canada, or other English-speaking countries. All other things being equal, the more dispersed the domestic franchising operations, the greater the monitoring capabilities, and the more likely the franchisor will seek international franchisees.

The geographic dispersion hypothesis can also be explained by the domestic saturation hypothesis. The greater the geographical scope of a franchising operation, the more likely the franchisor will exhaust domestic marketing opportunities, and thus the more likely it is to internationalize (Shane 1996b). Domestic saturation, therefore, can lead the franchisor to consider international opportunities for growth. Therefore,

H5: The greater the geographical dispersion of franchisees in the franchisor's system, the more likely the franchisor is to seek international franchisees.

Control Variables

Four variables are controlled for: (1) provisions of financing, (2) time, (3) start-up costs, and (4) industry. Provision of financing is controlled for because such arrangements in the international environment necessitate knowledge of capital markets and the legal environment. Shane (1996b) proposed that provision for financing can complicate international business relationships hindering the desire of these franchise systems to internationalize. On the demand side, however, financing options may entice a prospective foreign franchisee and, therefore, influence the franchisor to internationalize. Since provision of financing is a factor that may influence the decision of the franchisor to internationalize, this variable is taken into account.

Numerous researchers have pointed to a trend in the globalization of US franchising systems. However, it is not clear whether this trend is caused by firm-level variables or because of environmental or structural changes in the industries. For this reason, this study controls for time.

Start-up costs are controlled for because they constitute a major portion of the investment in a franchising system. Shane (1996b) stated that a negative relationship is expected between the start-up costs and the internationalization of the US franchisor because (1) capital markets are less efficient in foreign settings making it difficult to raise large sums of money, (2) high start-up costs make the franchising concept less desirable to potential foreign franchisees, and (3) it is more complicated to set up an expensive franchise contract. On the other hand, high start-up costs act as an additional price bond which, as predicted by the agency perspective, increase the likelihood of internationalization. Furthermore, the globalization of capital markets may moderate the effect of start-up costs on the decision to internationalize.

Huszagh et al. (1992) found that start-up costs were not a distinguishing factor between domestic and international franchisors in both 1967 and 1988 but asserted that start-up costs may re-emerge as a differentiating factor between domestic and international franchisors, and not because of the efficiency of capital markets. They theorized that downturns in the United States business cycle would diminish the ability of franchisors to sell their system domestically. Therefore, to maintain their growth rate, franchising systems will look for development abroad. Although not statistically significant, they observed that most of the internationalization efforts of US franchising systems in 1967 were in the lowest range of the start-up costs, while most of the internationalization activities of US franchising systems in 1988 were in the highest range.

Finally, industry is controlled for by focusing on retailing, professional business services, and hotels and motels separately. Industries are investigated separately because they use franchising in varying proportions, company characteristics and operating environments differ among industries, the effect of company capabilities on the decision to internationalize varies across industries, and there is a high multicollinearity between the industries and the predictor variables (See Shane 1996b). See table 3.1 for a summary of variables and hypotheses.

Table 3.1: Summary of Variables and Hypotheses

Hypotheses	Variable	Relationship
H1	Size	Positive
H2	Firm Age	Positive
H3	Growth	Positive
H4	Bonding	Negative
H5	Dispersion	Positive
Control Variables		
B6	Financing	
B7	Time	
B8	Start Cost	
B9	Franchise Age	

CONCLUSION

The model described in this chapter includes both resource-based and agency theories in the explanation of why franchisors internationalize. The decision to internationalize is dependent on the size, age, and growth rate, in addition to the price structure and the physical dispersion of the franchisor. The full model is illustrated in figure 3.1. In the next chapter, the research design which is used to test this model is developed.

Figure 3.1: The Model: Organizational Model of International Franchising

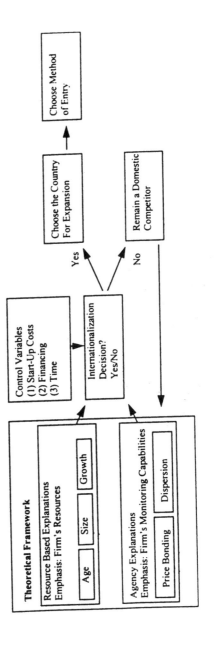

CHAPTER IV

Research Design

INTRODUCTION TO THE METHODOLOGY

In the previous chapter the hypotheses were developed. This chapter provides an overview of the methodology used in this study. This includes a review of the research questions, research hypotheses, data considerations, measurements of the constructs, and the statistical method used for data analysis. This study attempts to explain why franchisors internationalize using organizational explanations, or firm-level variables. Five hypotheses will be tested, three pertaining to the resource-based explanation of international franchising, and two relating to the agency perspective. These hypotheses are driven by the research questions which seek to find out why some franchisors within the same industry decide to explore foreign markets.

Data taken from *Entrepreneur* is used to test these hypotheses. The resource-based construct is measured by age, size, and growth, while the agency construct is measured by price bonding and physical dispersion. These measures were used in the past by franchising scholars. Finally, the statistical method is discussed. This discussion includes a rationale for using logistic regression, a short theoretical exposition of logistic regression, and comments on the interpretation of the logistic regression model.

METHODOLOGY

Research Questions

To facilitate understanding of international franchising, the following research questions were developed:
1) What firm characteristics of the franchisor are associated with international franchising expansion; and
2) How do these characteristics affect the desire of the franchisor to expand internationally.

Research Hypotheses

The following research hypotheses were developed:

Resource-based Theory

H1: The bigger the franchisor, the more likely it is to seek international franchisees.
H2: The older the franchisor, the more likely it is to seek international franchisees.
H3: The higher the growth of the franchising system, the more likely it is to seek international franchisees.

Agency Theory

H4: The greater the price bonding, the more likely the franchisor is to seek international franchisees.
H5: The greater the geographical dispersion of franchisees in the franchisor's system, the more likely the franchisor is to seek international franchisees.

International Franchising Data

Entrepreneur Magazine has published a "Franchise 500" survey in January of every year since 1980. According to the editors of the magazine, the "Franchise 500" listing is the best, most comprehensive and longest standing survey of franchises in the world. This data-set includes key firm characteristics of over 1000 franchisors. These characteristics include (1) the nature of the business, (2) the year the business began, (3) the year franchising began, (4) where the franchisor is seeking franchisees, (5) the number of franchisee and company-owned outlets, (6) the franchising fee, (7) the start-up costs, (8) the royalties, (9) the type of financing that is available, and (10) franchise 500 ranking.

This data set was used in both domestic franchising (Combs and Castrogiovanni 1994; Martin and Justis 1993) and international franchising (Shane 1996b) studies. Although the inclusion of franchisors in the survey is voluntary, several researchers have shown that no serious biases existed in the data (Castrogiovanni, Justis and Julien 1993; Combs and Castrogiovanni 1994). Combs and Castrogiovanni (1994) wrote that bias in the data appears minimal because "franchisors have considerable incentive to be listed since this is a good form of free advertising geared especially to their targeted audience, potential franchisees" (p. 42). Furthermore, the magazine itself validates about 80 percent of the data through the Uniform Franchise Offering Circular (UFOC), a prospectus required by US regulations which contains key information.

Dependent Variable

This study attempts to discover the factors that influence franchisors to internationalize. The dependent variable is the indication in *Entrepreneur* that the franchisors are seeking international franchising agreements. Shane (1996b) and Eroglu (1992) wrote that although intent to expand is not the same as actual expansion, this proxy is well suited for examining the internationalization of franchisors because (1) behavioral intentions often provide information on actual behavior, and (2) intended strategy provides information about the plans and strategies of the franchisor. The intention is real because *Entrepreneur* verifies most of the information against the UFOC.

Included in this measure is the desire to internationalize using master, direct international franchising, and joint venture agreements. This study, therefore, does not differentiate between the various modes of market entry.

Independent Variables

There are five predictor variables for the intentions of franchisors to internationalize: (1) size, (2) age, (3) growth, (4) bonding, and (5) dispersion. The size of the franchising system is measured using the firm's total number of units. The age of the franchising firm is measured using the number of years since inception. The growth rate was operationalized as the annual growth rate in the total number of units. These three measures—age, size and growth rate—have been used in the past literature as proxies of franchisor's resources (Carney and Gedajlovic 1991; Combs and Castrogiovanni 1994).

Bonding was operationalized by Shane (1996b, p. 80) as "the ratio of the initial franchise fee paid to the franchisor divided by the percentage royalty and advertising fee." As mentioned earlier, this pricing structure measured the amount of bonding because a high ratio would mean that the franchisee had high stakes. The order of the ongoing royalties to initial investment was reversed and measured as royalties divided by the initial fee. This allows the inclusion of franchisors which do not charge royalties at all, without making special assumptions. The zero point of the bonding variable is meaningful because it means that the franchisor is taking no financial risk and the entire payment for the franchising system is made initially. An advertising fee is not included in the price bonding variable because *Entrepreneur* has ceased collecting this data and advertising practices are different from one country to another. Finally, geographical dispersion is measured using a dummy variable indicating whether the franchisor is operating in all or some of the States.

Control Variables

As mentioned previously, four control variables are included: provision of financing, time, start-up costs and industry. Provision of financing is measured as a dummy variable indicating if financing is available. Because financing makes international operations more complex, Shane (1996b) proposed that a negative relationship exists between the presence of financing and the desire to internationalize.

The start-up costs are measured as all of the initial costs other than the franchise fee. Combs and Castrogiovanni (1994, p. 41) wrote that "high start-up costs suggest that the franchisee is the primary party risking loss of appropriable quasi-rents. These quasi-rents may actually provide an additional incentive for the franchisee to act in accordance with franchisor wishes in order to avoid quasi-rent appropriation."

The time variable is included to account for the trend in the internationalization of US franchising. A positive linear trend in internationalization is tested.

Finally, industry is controlled for by focusing on three service subsectors: retailing, professional business services, and hotels and motels. This is important because (1) industry variations are large in franchising (Castrogiovanni et al. 1995) and (2) the dummy variables for the industries exhibited high multicollinearity with the predictor variables (Shane 1996b). Table 4.1 provides a summary of the independent variables, control variables, measurements, and hypotheses.

Table 4.1: Measurement of the Variables and Hypotheses

Hypotheses	Variable	Measured as	Relationship
H1	Size	Total number of units	Positive
H2	Age	Number of years since firm began	Positive
H3	Growth	Percent change in number of units	Positive
H4	Bonding	Ongoing payments / Initial investment	Negative*
H5	Dispersion	0 = Some of the states 1 = All the states	Positive
Control Variables			
B6	Financing	0 = Not available 1 = Available	
B7	Time	Years	
B8	Start-Cost	$	
B9	Fran Age	Number of years since franchising began	

* = reverse coded to include additional observations

Statistical Method

The statistical method used in this study is logistic regression. The next section features (1) a rationale for using logistic regression, (2) a short theoretical exposition of logistic regression, and (3) comments on the interpretation of logistic regression.

Rational for Logistic Regression

This study examines the association between five independent (metric and nonmetric) variables and one nonmetric dependent variable, the decision to internationalize. Judge et al. (1980) wrote that quantal or discrete choice models "attempt to relate the conditional probability of a particular choice being made to various explanatory factors that include the attributes of the alternatives as well as the characteristics of the decision makers." These models are necessary because of problems arising from using ordinary least square regression procedures when analyzing discrete choices in the dependent variable. Judge et al. (1980) mentioned six reasons not to use ordinary linear regression models to analyze a discrete choice problem. First, the assumption of random error is violated because the random error can take only two values given the independent variables. Second, the assumption that the expected value of the error squared equals the variance is not tenable because the errors are heteroscedastic, resulting in inefficient estimates. Third, predictions outside the sample range are possible even when the conditional probability of the choice is confined to unit intervals. Fourth, fitted relationships will be sensitive to the value of the independent variables. Fifth, the R^2 measure is not meaningful because estimated errors are not consistent. Finally, since the dependent variable is not normally distributed, the linear methods of estimation are usually inefficient (Judge et al. 1980).

Hair et al. (1992, p. 62) wrote that "the researcher faced with a dichotomous variable need not resort to methods designed to accommodate the limitations of multiple regression. Logit analysis will address these problems and provide a method developed to deal directly with the situation in the most efficient manner possible." Logistical regression is a special form of regression which allows for a dichotomous dependent variable. This study uses logistical regression to evaluate the decision of franchisors to internationalize because (1) it allows for a binomial distribution of the error term, (2) it is able to incorporate linear and nonlinear effects, (3) it provides a wide range of diagnostics, (4) it is easy to interpret the coefficients, (5) it allows for metric and nonmetric independent variables (Hair et al. 1992), and (5) it was used by Shane (1996b) to analyze the determinants of international franchising expansion.

Theory of Logistic Regression

Logistical regression is similar to ordinary regression in the results but the method used to achieve these results is different (Hair et al. 1992). While ordinary regression often uses the least square method, logistic regression uses the maximum likelihood method of estimating the coefficients. This is because the cumulative logistic distribution function is non-linear in both the independent variables and the coefficients (Gujarati 1995). The equation for the logistic distribution function is:

(1) $Pi = 1/(1 + e^{Zi})$, where $Zi = BiXi$.

The natural log of the odds ratio, or the ratio between the probability that an event will occur and the probability that the event will not occur, provides the logit model. This model is specified as:

(2) $Li = \ln (Pi/(Pi - 1)) = Zi = BiXi$.

Gujarati (1995) noted five properties of the logit model. These are (1) as the probability moves from 0 and 1, the logit moves from negative infinity to positive infinity, (2) although L is linear in the independent variables the probabilities are not, (3) the coefficients indicate how the log-odds in favor of making the decision change as the independent variables change by one unit and the intercept is the log-odds in favor of making the decision when the independent variables are zero, (4) the probability of an event occurring can be calculated directly from equation 1, and (5) the log-odds ratio is assumed to be linearly related to the independent variables.

Interpretation of Logistic Regression Analysis

Logistic regression provides the probability that an event will occur or not occur. Thus, if the prediction is 0.50 or above, the prediction is yes, and if it is below 0.50 the prediction is no. The sign of the coefficient is interpreted in a similar fashion to the sign of a normal regression analysis. That is, a positive coefficient increases the predicted probability while a negative one decreases the probability of an event occurring. If Bi is positive, the antilog is more than one and odds will be increasing. A coefficient of zero means that no change is taking place in the odds (Hair et al. 1992).

As mentioned earlier, the R^2 is not helpful in determining the fit of the model. An alternative method of estimating the model is the likelihood value. This is calculated as -2 times the log of the likelihood model (-2LL). The interpretation is opposite the one used by the R^2. The lower -2LL, the better the fit of the model. The minimum value of -2LL is zero (Hair et al. 1992). The -2LL measure follows a chi-squared distribution. Two other methods to assess the overall fit of the model are classification table and chi-square. The chi-squared test, analogous to the F-test in ordinary regressions, checks whether the difference between the log of likelihood with and without the independent variables is statistically significant. It shows whether the independent variables collectively add information to the model (Menard 1995).

CONCLUSION

The objectives of this study are two fold: (1) to determine the company factors associated with the internationalization of US franchisors, and (2) to find the relationships between these factors and the decision to internationalize. To achieve these objectives, logistic regression analysis is used on the data set provided by *Entrepreneur*. This data set gives information about the companies and their desire to seek international franchisees. The desire to internationalize is shown as a discrete choice. Logistic regression is a method designed to accommodate analysis of dichotomous dependent variables. Using cross sectional data, this method was previously used by Shane (1996b) to determine the effects of company specific variables on the intention of US franchisors to internationalize. Since this study examines the same phenomenon using a similar data set, logistic regression should prove to be an efficient and effective method of analysis.

CHAPTER V

Data Analysis

INTRODUCTION

This chapter provides the results for each industry, resulting in three models. In this section, descriptive statistics including mean, minimum, maximum and standard deviation for each of the models are given. Correlation matrices of the independent variables for each of the industries are shown. The Wald statistic was used to test the coefficients in each model. The Wald statistic follows a normal distribution and parallels the t-ratio test employed in ordinary least square regressions (Menard 1995). This chi-squared statistic was used to check the overall fit of the models.

Heteroskedasticity tests were performed on each of the models. These tests are designed to check whether the variance is constant across all values. While the coefficients remain unbiased in the presence of heteroskedasticity, they are not the most efficient (McClendon 1994). Therefore, it is important to determine whether heteroskedasticity exists. White's test of heteroskedasticity is used because it is not as dependent on the assumption of normality as some of the other tests (McClendon 1994).

Modifications of the original model were made to empirically test the models. There was a multicollinearity problem between firm age and the age of the franchise. Since the age of the firm was used to measure the firm's resources and the age of the franchise was used as a control variable, the age of the franchise was removed from the model. High correlations among the independent variables will still result in unbiased and efficient estimates of logistic regression coefficients, but the standard deviation of the coefficient will tend to be larger, resulting in failure to reject the null hypotheses when the null hypothesis should be rejected (Menard 1995). Logistical regression analyses were applied to the data set with and without the age of the franchising system and it was found that the latter provided better results. The model without the age of the franchise system was used throughout to allow for statistical comparisons between the industries.

The original sample included 725 observations. Because of missing variables on some of the observations, 132 observations were deleted, about 18 percent of the data. To test the robustness of the model's logistical regressions with expanded samples were also tested. This was done by extrapolating variables for missing observations and controlling for this procedure through an additional dummy variable. Since no significant changes occurred in the coefficients, the original models were retained.

RETAIL SECTOR ANALYSIS

Retail businesses have approached internationalization with caution. It was not until the 1970s that some of the biggest retailing businesses in Europe and the United States internationalized (Daniels 1993). Simpson and Thorpe (1995) reported that 38 percent of specialty stores and 21 percent of general merchandise retailers globalized their operations. International franchising companies in retailing can be thought of as associations of locally-owned businesses working under the operating umbrella of the franchisor. This allows a small consumer-oriented firm to take advantage of the regulatory structure of a small firm and the economies of scale of a multinational company (Feketekuty 1988).

Daniels (1993) stated that the success of retailers abroad is dependent on the their ability to provide a marketing mix that matches multinational consumers' expectations of consumers in different cultural contexts. The highly specialized niche players, such as the Body Shop, Benetton, and Marks & Spencer, serving a restricted market, seem most successful in adapting to different environmental contexts. Similarly, Simpson and Thorpe (1995) wrote that the success of a franchisor in a foreign market is dependent on the extent of product differentiation, the compatability match between the store and the lifestyle of local consumers, the projected image of the store, and the possession of a distinct market niche. Huszagh et al. (1992) proposed that retailing franchise systems that reflect the US life style are more likely to succeed abroad, especially in the early stages. "The line of reasoning here is that, in the late 1960s, international franchisors' product/service offerings which compared with domestic franchisors would be more reflective of American lifestyle concepts" (Huszagh et al. 1992, p. 9). They used the early internationalization of restaurant franchising in the 1970s to support this point.

In the retailing industry, economies of scale in purchasing, planning, and controlling resulted in cost savings to the firm. These cost savings translate to higher profits and more resources available for international expansion. The advantage of economies of scale in retailing is demonstrated by the growth of multi-establishment firms such as Blockbuster, Seven Eleven, McDonalds, and Baskin-Robins (Feketekuty 1988). "The organizational development of large retail operations has facilitated functional specialisation within retailing, which in turn has contributed to retailers' improved capacity to exploit international opportunities" (Akehurst and Alexander 1995, p. 4).

Results of the Retailing Model

The retail sector included 367 observations of 158 companies. Table 5.1 shows the descriptive statistics of the independent variables and the correlations among them. The retail logistical model is shown in table 5.2. The model provides support for both resource-based and agency hypotheses.

Table 5.1: Descriptive Statistics and Correlations of Independent Variables for the Retail Sector

Dependent Variable: Mean = 0.25886; SD = 0.43860; 0 (Domestic) = 272; 1 (Inter) = 95

n = 367	size X1	age X2	growth X3	bonding X4	dispersion X5	financing X6	time X7	start cost X8	fran age X9
min	0	1	-0.875	0	0	0	0	0	1
max	6,705	119	22	1	1	1	7	975.5	69
mean	184.0444	17.8000	0.5902	0.2632	0.6222	0.2797	3.4395	138.3074	9.4568
sd	438.6439	19.0757	1.9437	0.0899	0.4872	0.4377	2.3744	142.9466	11.4471

	Size	Frage	Grow	Bond	Disper	Fin	Age	Time	Start
Size	1.000								
Age	.34224	1.000							
Grow	-.0276	-.1827	1.000						
Bond	-.0026	-.2304	.04042	1.000					
Disper	.16448	.18529	.01444	-.0601	1.000				
Fin	.02613	.11507	-.0197	.09361	.01587	1.000			
Frage	.32094	**.82885**	-.1341	-.2046	.06252	.09333	1.000		
Time	.05220	.04984	.01481	-.0089	.16103	.28620	.02606	1.000	
Start	.15417	.52566	-.0568	-.2993	.19404	.04076	.46562	.08288	1.000

Table 5.2: The Retail Logistical Model

Iterations-5

Log-likelihood -189.663002

Log-likelihood with only a constant term -209.871332

Chi-squared (8) = 40.417 @ Prob = 0.00000

Variable		Hypotheses	Coefficient	Std. Error	T-ratio
Constant			-1.50666	0.44340	-3.3980
H1	Size	Positive	0.00053	0.00027	1.9315
H2	Age	Positive	-0.02483	0.01117	-2.2223
H3	Growth	Positive	0.12345	0.06764	1.8251
H4	Bonding	Negative	-0.41253	0.80522	-0.5123
H5	Dispersion	Positive	1.01248	0.29603	3.4202
Control Variables					
B6	Financing		0.86978	0.29224	2.9762
B7	Time		-0.00711	0.05855	-0.1214
B8	Start Costs		-0.00096	0.00109	-0.8827

Bold = significant at .10 level

Resource-Based Theory

The resource-based theory appears to provide information on whether a franchisor will decide to internationalize. The size of the firm is significant and positively related to the decision of franchisors to internationalize. Likewise, the growth in the number of outlets is also significant and positively related to the franchisor's intention to internationalize. Bigger and faster-growing firms may have more resources which would allow them to expand overseas. These results are consistent with the hypothesized relationships.

Although the age of the firm is significant, the coefficient reveals a negative relationship to the dependent variable. According to this result, younger retailing firms are more likely to internationalize than older ones, *ceteris paribus*. This result may be partly because of the fact that (1) younger firms are more adventurous and willing to take chances with their franchise system overseas, and (2) start up franchising companies are more aggressive in recruiting foreign franchisees for the purpose of collecting franchising fees.

The explanation of the age variable may be industry-related. High levels of domestic market saturation in the retailing sector may drive a franchisor to seek opportunities for growth overseas early in its life cycle. The forces which have motivated the internationalization of retailers are: (1) saturated and highly competitive national markets, (2) slow population growth in most developed markets, (3) little innovation in the domestic market because of planning controls, and (4) restrictive domestic regulatory environment (Daniels 1993). Given these constraints in the domestic environment, it is no wonder that more and more retailers are seeking expansion through international franchisees early in their life cycle.

Agency Theory

The logistic retailing model also provides support for one of the agency theory variables. Both of the hypothesized relationships have the expected sign in the coefficient but only the dispersion variable is significant. There is a negative but insignificant relationship between the price bonding and the decision to internationalize. However, this relationship may be a reflection of random sampling error.

Unlike Shane's (1996b) study, the price bonding variable was not significant for this model. The inability to confirm Shane's (1996b) results may be attributable to the fact that each industry was isolated and examined overtime. Shane's model covered all franchising and was cross-sectional. The geographical scope of the franchisor is the most significant variable in the model. As hypothesized, it is positively related to the decision to internationalize. Physical dispersion within the United States may allow the franchisor to develop the monitoring systems necessary for overseas expansion.

Control Variables

In the retail logistical model, financing options were significant and positively related to the internationalization of these franchising systems. This may be the case because attractive financing terms entice prospective franchisees from overseas. Therefore, the demand for United States franchising may play an important role in the decision of retailers to expand their franchising systems abroad. The relationship between time and the internationalization of franchising systems was found to be negative and insignificant. It seems that the trend toward internationalization over time has been accounted for at least partly by changes in the franchisors' organizational characteristics. The trend of internationalization may be a result of maturity in the product life cycle of the franchising industry. Finally, the coefficient for start-up costs was negative and insignificant in relation to the intention to internationalize.

Robustness

White's test of heteroskedasticity revealed a slight problem of heteroskedasticity in the retailing logistical regression model. The chi-squared value of the model (26.27) exceeded the chi-squared critical value (15.51) at (= .05. This means that the homoskedasticity assumption can not be accepted. To evaluate the magnitude of the heteroskedasticity, the coefficient of variability, or the standard deviation of a variable divided by its mean, was employed (McClendon 1994). The coefficient of variability shows that the heteroskedasticity of the error variance is about 1.24 larger than the constant error variance under the homoskedasticity assumption. Because the magnitude of the problem is not large and because correcting for heteroskedasticity will not necessarily improve the results, the original model is retained.

Summary

For the retailing sector, there is some evidence for both the resource-based and agency hypotheses. The model chi-square is highly significant at p=0.00000. This test parallels the global F-test in ordinary least square regressions. The model predicted over 75.48 percent of the cases accurately.

HOTEL AND MOTEL SECTOR ANALYSIS

The hotel industry is the most mature industry of the three, with an average of 813 establishments per franchisor. The internationalization of hotel and motel chains started in the 1950s and 1960s with firms such as Hilton, Sheraton, Holiday Inn, Marriott and Ramada Inn. Following the product life cycle theory, since they are more mature, hotel and motel chains have internationalized early and currently have the highest levels of internationalization among the three industries. Hotel and motel chains have globalized their operations partly because of higher competition and declining profits in the US market (Huszagh et al. 1992).

Kostecka (1988) proposed that an increase in the internationalization of certain service franchise systems may be partly related to the magnitude of tourism from the United States. The internationalization of the hotel industry is motivated in part by the mobile (foot-loose) consumer base and tourism (Tucker and Sundberg 1988). Davies and Fergusson (1995) wrote that many of the Japanese hotel developments in Hong Kong and Singapore were built to cater to the Japanese consumer. Therefore, for the hotel industry, the geographical scope of travelers from the home country may be an important determinant in choosing the country for internationalization.

Results of the Hotel and Motel Model

The hotel and motel category included 69 observations of 30 firms. Descriptive statistics of the independent variables and the correlations are in table 5.3. The model is in table 5.4. The hotel and motel model shows support for both the resource-based and agency perspectives.

Table 5.3: Descriptive Statistics and Correlations of Independent Variables for the Hotel and Motel Sector

Dependent Variable: Mean = 0.71014; SD = 0.45702; 0 (Domestic) = 20; 1 (Inter) = 49

n = 69	size X1	age X2	growth X3	bonding X4	dispersion X5	financing X6	time X7	start cost X8	fran age X9
min	0	1	-0.2	0.001463	0	0	0	1.65	1
max	3353	60	4	0.35	1	1	7	12000	58
mean	529.72	24.754	0.26102	0.15059	0.91304	0.17391	3.058	1904	17.116
sd	813.14	20.669	0.55263	0.059575	0.28384	0.38181	2.3002	2517	16.099

	Size	Frage	Grow	Bond	Disper	Fin	Age	Time	Start
Size	1.000								
Age	.85920	1.000							
Grow	-.1517	-.2274	1.000						
Bond	.19425	-.3242	.01555	1.000					
Disper	.00603	.01189	-.0908	.07836	1.000				
Fin	.34075	.17448	-.1487	-.0822	.02780	1.000			
Frage	.56048	.74923	-.2502	-.0150	.08152	.01484	1.000		
Time	.21345	.10505	-.2448	-.0631	-.1723	.47644	.00370	1.000	
Start	.02762	.03405	-.0632	-.2420	.03341	.14006	-.0828	-.0793	1.000

Table 5.4: The Hotel and Motel Logistical Model

Iterations-6
Log-likelihood -30.158154
Log-likelihood with only a constant term -41.539509
Chi-squared (8) = 22.763 @ Prob = 0.00368

Variable		Hypotheses	Coefficient	Std. Error	T-ratio
Constant			-0.32783	1.96439	-0.1669
H1	Size	Positive	0.00205	0.00100	2.0542
H2	Age	Positive	0.01883	0.02010	0.9364
H3	Growth	Positive	2.94872	1.57179	1.8760
H4	Bonding	Negative	-8.98498	5.70390	-1.5752
H5	Dispersion	Positive	1.97279	1.56536	1.2603
Control Variables					
B6	Financing		-0.57466	0.89463	-0.6425
B7	Time		-0.17306	0.16323	-1.0602
B8	Start Costs		-0.00009	0.00012	-0.7325

Bold = significant at .10 level

Resource-Based Theory

As in the case of the retailing sector, both the size of the firm and the growth rate of the franchising systems are positively related to the hotel and motel franchising system's intention to internationalize. Bigger and faster-growing hotel and motel chains have more resources and, therefore, are more likely to internationalize. The coefficient for the age of the firm was positive as expected, but insignificant. To check whether this was due to the high correlations between age and size, an additional regression was run without the size variable. The results revealed a strong positive relationship ($t=2.2870$) between the age of the firm and its intentions to internationalize. The rest of the coefficients remained approximately the same.

Agency Theory

The logistical model for the hotel and motel sector shows some support for the agency perspective. The study of this industry agrees with Shane's finding that the greater the price bonding, the more likely the franchisor will internationalize. As mentioned earlier, this is because the greater the franchise fee relative to the royalty rates, the more the franchisee has to lose. Therefore, the franchisor is ensured that the foreign franchisee will abide by the franchise agreement and is more likely to internationalize its franchising operation. The domestic dispersion of the franchising operation is mildly significant ($t = 1.26$). It is positively related to the decision to internationalize as the theory predicts.

Control Variables

Financing, time, and start-up costs were controlled for. The Wald statistic shows that none of the null hypotheses can be rejected for any of the control variables. As in the retailing case, it seems that most of the significant variations in the dependent variable are accounted for by the independent variables.

Robustness

To check the robustness of the coefficients, an expanded sample which extrapolated missing values for start-up costs using the sample mean was also regressed. A dummy variable was used to control for this extrapolation. This procedure allowed for the inclusion of 24 additional cases. There was no significant change in the structure of the model, so the original model was retained. White's test of heteroskedasticity revealed no such problem in the present model.

Summary

The model provides support for both the resource-based and agency theory approaches. All of the signs of the coefficients were in the same direction as these theories predict. The size, growth and price bonding variables were all significantly related to the decision to internationalize, and in the direction which the model predicted. As expected, the coefficient for the dispersion variable was positive, but its relationship to the dependent variable was weak. Finally, the age coefficient was positive but insignificant. The chi-squared statistic indicate a statistically significant fit between all of the variables and the decision to internationalize (Prob = 0.00368). The model predicted 78.26 percent of the observations correctly.

PROFESSIONAL BUSINESS SERVICES ANALYSIS

The internationalization of business services is a recent phenomenon which started in the 1960s but did not gain momentum until the 1980s. In the beginning, most of the demand for business services came from big businesses. This is why the internationalization of professional business services paralleled the internationalization of their industrial clients (Noyelle and Dutka 1988). Advances in telecommunications and information systems made it feasible to centralize the production of business services, especially the ones requiring specialized inputs. (Feketekuty 1988). This allowed for the international expansion of professional business services. "The same economic forces that led to the growth of national firms and to the centralization of business services within countries have also led to the growth of international firms and to the centralization of some business services at an international level" (Feketekuty 1988, p. 52). The internationalization of professional business services from the 1960s to the 1980s has been influenced primarily by the economics of the firm-client relationship and has been limited to very big firms (Noyelle and Dutka 1988). These firms have moved into new countries in response to the needs of their clients.

The structure of the industry is changing. More and more small and medium sized companies are now demanding professional business services. This has led to the development of many market-niches and the creation of new strategies to capture these niches. "Rather than having the demand of large corporations structure the supply of business service firms, the latter must now structure the demand for their services. Indeed, there is evidence of a shift whereby regional, national, or multinational expansion is increasingly guided by the business service firm's assessment of the potential of these new, mostly local markets, less by the demand of the large national or multinational corporations." (Noyelle and Dutka 1988, p. 28). It is this latter group of businesses that comprises the data set in this study. They are relatively young (16 years old) niche players, that serve small to medium-sized businesses. Therefore, their internationalization may be dependent on firm-level variables, and not as much on environmental variables. Noyelle and Dutka (1988) estimated that the world market for advertising services, management consulting, and accounting firms was $20 billion, $20 billion, and $40 billion, respectively.

Huszagh et al. (1992) found a high rate of growth in the internationalization of business services and attributed it to (1) positive image of "made in the US" services, and (2) higher technological content in the production of these services. Feketekuty (1988) stated that increased competition in global manufacturing raised the need to acquire the best international business services. Noyelle and Dutka (1988) wrote that international demand for business services grew in response to changing business conditions and the realization that these professional business services have the potential to streamline work, provide better controls, and expand opportunities for larger profits. They also added that the internationalization of business services parallels the increasing externalization of business services among manufacturing firms. "Such contracted expertise was likely to be better and ultimately cheaper than in-house expertise" (Noyelle and Dutka 1988, p. 28).

There are a number of impediments to the internationalization of professional business services. These include (1) cultural differences, (2) restrictions on the mobility of personnel, (3) restrictions on the transfer of technology (Feketekuty 1988), (4) national procurement policies, and (5) professional licensing issues (Noyelle and Dutka 1988). While these impediments are not unique to the internationalization of business services, they impose a great difficulty on the delivery of a professional business service in a host country. This is partly because professional business services require high levels of human capital input. Therefore, limitations on travel and the practice of accountants in host countries, for example, can severely affect the ability of these professionals to deliver a quality service in these countries. Manufacturing firms may be able to circumvent some of these impediments to internationalization through a change in the method of entry. For example, manufacturers can export their product or license their technology. These changes are not readily available for professional business services.

Results of the Professional Business Service Model

The professional business service category included 156 observations of 71 firms. See table 5.5 for the descriptive statistics and the correlations. Table 5.6 features the model for the professional business services category.

Table 5.5: Descriptive Statistics and Correlations of Independent Variables for the Professional Business Service Sector

Dependent Variable: Mean = 0.28205; SD = 0.45145; 0 (Domestic) = 112; 1 (Inter) = 44

$n = 156$	size X1	age X2	growth X3	bonding X4	dispersion X5	financing X6	time X7	start cost X8	fran age X9
min	1	1	-0.75	0	0	0	0	0	2
max	1448	63	21	1	1	1	7	117.5	62
mean	115.5340	15.9750	0.5550	0.3405	0.7010	0.4460	3.6760	20.4120	10.8980
sd	200.4838	12.4951	1.8700	0.2630	0.4577	0.4983	2.4082	19.1316	10.7900

	Size	Frage	Grow	Bond	Disper	Fin	Age	Time	Start
Size	1.000								
Age	.54602	1.000							
Grow	-.1204	-.1917	1.000						
Bond	-.2319	-.1286	.07235	1.000					
Disper	.27721	.09219	-.0990	-.1433	1.000				
Fin	.23479	.12437	.08179	.01280	.16757	1.000			
Frage	.54191	.84431	-.2053	-.2064	.13262	.06967	1.000		
Time	.00723	.03431	.12152	-.1255	-.3090	.18696	.08532	1.000	
Start	-.0138	.11014	.28861	.04729	.16648	-.0858	.12048	.09528	1.000

Table 5.6: The Professional Business Services Logistical Model

Iterations-4
Log-likelihood -84.442153
Log-likelihood with only a constant term -92.801320
Chi-squared (8) = 16.718 @ Prob = 0.03318

Variable		Hypotheses	Coefficient	Std. Error	T-ratio
Constant			-1.72420	.68193	-2.5284
H1	Size	Positive	0.00327	0.00160	2.0427
H2	Age	Positive	-0.00507	0.01685	-0.3007
H3	Growth	Positive	0.14408	0.16352	0.8811
H4	Bonding	Negative	-0.22021	0.82895	-0.2657
H5	Dispersion	Positive	0.30758	0.51922	0.5924
Control Variables					
B6	Financing		-0.40933	0.42472	-0.9638
B7	Time		-0.00177	0.08912	-0.0199
B8	Start Costs		0.02221	0.01084	2.0494

Bold = significant at .10 level

Unlike the previous two models for the retailing and hotel industries, the professional business service model does not show strong evidence for most of the independent variables. Except for size and start-up costs, the model failed to reject the other null hypotheses. The reasons for this may be empirical or substantive. In this study, the percentage of professional business service franchises that internationalized was nine percent, resulting in only 14 firms. This means that there was little variation in the dependent variable. The implications are that (1) significant variables are probably highly related to the dependent variable, and (2) statistically insignificant variables may still be related to the dependent variable. Therefore, it is possible that if there was more variation in the dependent variable, the rest of the independent variables would also become significant.

From a substantive standpoint, several reasons may have contributed to the results. The high levels of human capital necessary in the production of professional business services may discourage franchisors to internationalize. This is especially true if these resources are unavailable in the host country. Furthermore, the limitations on the internationalization of professional business services that were mentioned earlier may also impede internationalization. Therefore, it is not until the firm develops its own resources as it grows that it attempts to globalize its operations.

Resource-Based Theory

The size of the business service franchisor was positively and significantly related to the intention of franchisors to internationalize. Why did the size of the professional business franchise systems emerge as a significant variable? Larger networks of professional business services may provide these businesses with brand-name recognition and an image of professionalism that is unmatched by smaller systems. The size of the franchising system is important in establishing new clientele domestically, and even more so internationally, because less information is available to prospective clients. Therefore, the size of the franchise system may act as an entry barrier to new firms in international markets. In addition, Huszagh et al. (1992) claimed that bigger firms may be able to secure capital in foreign countries more easily.

"In services, perhaps even more so than in goods, clients have very limited means for assessing the quality and usefulness of the product that they are purchasing until they have indeed done so. Service firms must invest considerable resources in building their reputations and in enhancing their clients' trust in the professionalism of their work" (Noyelle and Dutka 1988, p. 48). One way to do that is through the establishment of large network systems. The establishment of large networks of professional business services became necessary to the formation of unique linkages with clients that competitors could not easily replicate (Noyelle and Dutka 1988). The increase in the size of the professional business services permits the firm to centralize the production of some services, resulting in cost savings, and to communicate a message of professionalism, allowing it to compete globally.

The age variable was shown to be negative and insignificant. To check whether this result was due to the high correlations between the size and the age variable, a regression was run without the size variable. The results showed a weak positive relationship (t=1.0349) between the age variable and the decision to internationalize.

Control Variables

An interesting result that emerged from the professional business services model is that the control variable for start-up costs was highly significant and positively related to the decision to internationalize. This result can be explained using the agency perspective. Combs and Castrogiovanni (1994, p. 41) wrote that "high start-up costs suggest that the franchisee is the primary party risking loss of appropriable quasi-rents. These quasi-rents may actually provide an additional incentive for the franchisee to act in accordance with franchisor wishes in order to avoid quasi-rent appropriation." Since start-up costs increase the bonding between the franchisee and franchisor, the franchisor is more likely to internationalize when there are higher start-up costs. The significance of the start-up cost variable is consistent with Huszagh et al.'s (1992) prediction that the equity capital requirements of the franchisor will re-emerge as a significant factor distinguishing between domestic and international franchisors.

Robustness

To test the robustness of the coefficients, several models were checked. The price bonding variable was extrapolated by using sample means and adding a dummy variable to account for this procedure. This technique allowed the inclusion of 42 observations to the sample. Also, a model was regressed which included the age of the franchise. The results were consistent with the original model in both cases. White's test showed no problem of heteroskedasticity in the data.

Summary

Three aspects of the model show promise. The model predicted 78.21 percent of the cases accurately. This accuracy is comparable to the previous models. It accurately identified 85.71 percent of the business services that internationalized. All the coefficients had the expected sign. Finally, as expected by the resource based hypothesis, the coefficient for the size variable is highly significant and positively related to the dependent variable. The bigger the franchisor, the more likely it will seek international franchisees. The model for the professional business service category provides strong evidence that, taken collectively, the independent and control variables provide useful information about the intentions of the franchisor to internationalize its operations. The chi-squared test is significant at Prob = 0.03.

CONCLUSION

The research shows that both resources and monitoring capabilities are necessary to explain international franchising. All of the models were statistically significant. This is consistent with Fladmoe-Lindquist's (1996) research that theorized that the internationalization of US franchisors was partly a result of agency and resource-based explanations. Shane (1996b) empirically tested the agency theory perspective and found evidence to support it. This study provides evidence that the firms' resources may also affect the decision of franchisors to internationalize.

However, the empirical results on the effect of resources on the decision to internationalize may be due to spurious correlation between the independent variables—in particular the size and the growth-rate of the firm—and the dependent variable. The size and the growth-rate of the franchisor may be partly influenced by its decision to internationalize. Therefore, the results for the coefficients of the resource-based explanations should be interpreted with caution.

This study also supports the idea that empirical investigations of franchising should be conducted on an industry by industry basis. This is because these industries have different structures and dissimilarities in the predictors of internationalization. The internationalization of retailing, hotels and motels, and professional business services are grounded in different environmental explanations. Retailers globalize their operations to capitalize on the consumer base of different nations by developing highly specialized market niches. Hotels internationalize in response to changes in tourism and the hospitality industry in the host country. Oftentimes, their internationalization is motivated by the traveling needs of home-country residents. Early internationalization of professional business services paralleled the internationalization of their clients. This trend is changing as more business service firms develop market segments in the community which cater particularly to the small to medium sized firms of the host country. The differing contexts of the internationalization process of the three industries demonstrate the importance of studying each industry separately.

Summary and Conclusions

INTRODUCTION

Chapter VI includes a discussion of the results. A discussion of each hypothesis is provided. This is followed by a conclusion, implications to practitioners, and the possibility for future research. The discussion of the hypotheses reveals strong similarities in the organizational determinants of international franchising for all three industries. However, the effect of the independent variables on the decision to internationalize varied by industry, and the vectors of independent variables are shown to be significantly different, as indicated by the log likelihood test. The conclusion of this paper is that both resource-based and agency theories contribute to the understanding of the globalization efforts of franchisors in three industries. Practitioners in these industries can use the data to assess their competitive stance *vis-à-vis* other industry players. This information should also prove to be useful to franchisees and portfolio investors who are considering investing in the franchising system. This is because internationalization may affect the success of the overall system in the long run.

COMPARISONS OF THE HYPOTHESES

Table 6.1 shows a comparison of the coefficients of the results for the three industries. Overall, with the exception of age, the signs of the coefficients for the independent variables are consistent with the model developed in this study. In the next section, a comparison of each hypothesis is made.

Table 6.1: Comparisons of Three Industrial Sectors

Variable		Hypotheses	Retail	Hotels	Professional Bus Services
H1	Size	Positive	Positive	Positive	Positive
H2	Age	Positive	Negative	Positive	Negative
H3	Growth	Positive	Positive	Positive	Positive
H4	Bonding	Negative	Negative	Negative	Negative
H5	Dispersion	Positive	Positive	Positive	Positive
Control Variables					
B6	Financing		Positive	Negative	Negative
B7	Time		Negative	Negative	Negative
B8	Start Costs		Negative	Negative	Positive

Bold = significant at p = .10

Hypothesis One: Size

The size of the franchising system is the only variable that emerged as significant in all of the three cases. The size of the franchising system is positively related to the probability of internationalization of retail, hotel and motel, and professional business services. The size of the firm influences the economies of scale and the experience of the firm (Huszagh et al. 1992). Both contribute to the human and physical capital of the franchisor, and to the accumulation of resources in general. As the number of outlets a franchising system owns increases, so do the economies of scale, experience, and monitoring capabilities. These factors provide firms with the intellectual and monetary resources needed for international expansion. The more resources the franchising firm has, the more likely it is that it will seek international franchisees. Furthermore, saturation in the market can also explain why bigger firms are more likely to seek internationalization.

Hypothesis Two: Age

The age variable showed mixed results. Contrary to the premise of this study, the retailing sector revealed a negative association between the age of the franchisor and its intention to internationalize. For the hotel and business service industries, the sign of the coefficient was positive and negative, respectively, and in both cases the coefficient was insignificant. However, when the size variable was eliminated from the regressions of the hotel and business services, the age variable became positive and significant. This is because of the high correlation between the size and the age variables in these industries.

There are a number of explanations that may have contributed to the negative coefficient in the retailing sector. It is possible that younger franchising firms may be ignorant of the risks involved in international expansion. Therefore, their decision to internationalize from the very start may be a result of their daring nature and the desire on their part to collect franchisee fees from their foreign affiliates. Another explanation for these results can emerge from examining different types of franchisors. Using factor analysis, Carney and Gedajlovic (1991) found five types of franchisors: (1) rapid growers, (2) conservative expansive, (3) franchise converts, (4) mature franchises, and (5) unsuccessfuls. It is the first group of franchisors that may have contributed to the insignificance of the age variable in hotel and business service models, and seemingly inconsistent results for the retailing sector. This group of franchisors is young (franchising for 4.1 years), large (156.7 units), low priced (125K total investment), and very fast growing (53.3 outlets per year). They also seek growth overseas early in their life cycle. Carney and Gedajlovic (1991, p. 615) wrote that "the expansion objectives of the rapid growers extend beyond the boundaries of their home province." Some young companies may have a global product which requires rapid internationalization early in the life cycle of the franchisor.

Hypothesis Three: Growth Rate

The coefficients for the growth rate were positive in all three models as well as the combined model. They were significant in all of the models, except for the professional business services. Therefore, the greater the growth rate in the total number of outlets of a franchisor, the more likely it was to seek international franchisees. When the results of the growth rate are taken together with the results for the size of the franchising system, more evidence is accumulated for the resource-based explanation of international franchising. Bigger and faster-growing firms have more resources and are more likely to seek international franchisees.

Hypothesis Four: Price Bonding

As expected by the agency theory, the price bonding coefficients are negative for all the models. The greater the price bond, the more likely that the franchisor will internationalize. However, the price bonding variable is only significant for the hotel and motel industry. The insignificance of the results of the price bonding coefficient for the retail and professional business services may be the result of data problems. The data set does not differentiate between the price structure of the franchise system for domestic and international prospective franchisees. As such the variation in the price structure can only be observed across companies and not within companies.

Although Shane (1996b) was faced with the same data limitation, his empirical investigation supported the price bonding variable. Shane (1996b) combined all industries in his analysis. Therefore, the price bonding variable may have become significant partly because of industry variations. For example, this study revealed that the price bonding ratio and start-up costs for the hotel industry is the highest of the three industries studied. Thus, the price structure of hotels is most suitable for international expansion. This industry is also the most global in scope. Because Shane (1996b) combined all industries in his model, inter-industry variations in the price structure strengthened the statistical association he found. Since the present study investigates the intra-industry variations in the price structure and data are limited at the company level, the results do not unanimously support Shane's (1996b) findings.

Given the data limitations, the fact that the sign of the coefficients for the price bonding agrees with the premise of this study for all three industries is promising. Furthermore, the hotel and motel model provides the most support for Shane's (1996b) theory regarding the effect of the price structure on the franchising firm's decision to internationalize. Finally, there is evidence in the literature that indicates that this relationship should hold. A survey by Arthur Andersen (1996) found that franchisors tend to charge higher initial fees and lower ongoing fees to the foreign affiliates in comparison to their domestic ones. And this was shown to be true in general, and for the industries discussed in this study. It is also true for different modes of entry, including master franchising, direct franchising, and area development franchising. Therefore, it is believed that the higher the price bonding in the price structure of the franchisor, the more likely it is that it will seek international franchisees, masters, and area developers.

Hypothesis Five: Dispersion

The geographical scope of operation has a positive effect on the decision to internationalize in all three models, including the combined model. However, it is only significant for the retailing sector. The significance of this variable for the retailing sector may be indicative of the importance of developing monitoring skills in the domestic context. The fact that the signs of the coefficients agree with the hypothesized relationships in all the models and are significant in the retailing model may provide support for the agency explanation of international franchising. Dispersion in the domestic market may necessitate that franchising firms develop sophisticated monitoring systems of their franchisees. This positions them advantageously for international expansion. Furthermore, the greater the geographical scope of the operation, the greater the likelihood of domestic saturation. As mentioned earlier, market saturation in the retailing sector may have contributed to the internationalization of retail franchise systems.

A Global Test for the Structure of the Coefficients

In order to check whether the vectors of the independent variable are the same, a logistical model was regressed on the data set which combined all three industries. Descriptive statistics and correlations are in table 6.2.

The combined logistical model is presented in table 6.3. This model predicted 72.30 percent of the observations accurately; the sign of the coefficient is mostly consistent with the three models, and the chi-squared test is significant at Prob = 0.00000. The chi-squared test was used to check for the significance of the changes in the log-likelihood. The chi-squared test of the log-likelihood shows that the vectors of independent variables are significantly different (Chi-Squared = 66.72). This means that the vectors of independent variable coefficients of all three models are significantly different from combined model.

Table 6.2: Descriptive Statistics and Correlations of Independent Variables for the Retail Sector

Dependent Variable: Mean = 0.31757; SD = 0.4592; 0 (Domestic) = 404; 1 (Inter) = 188

n = 592	size X1	firm age X2	growth X3	bonding X4	dispersion X5	financing X6	time X7	start cost X8	fran age X9
min	0	1	-0.875	0	0	0	0	0	1
max	6705	119	22	1	1	1	7	12000	69
mean	177.13	17.709	0.5441	0.26161	0.67568	0.30405	3.4088	314.78	10.748
sd	518.52	17.746	1.8005	0.19538	0.46852	0.46039	2.3555	1038.8	12.177
	Size	Frage	Grow	Bond	Disper	Fin	Age	Time	Start
Size	1.000								
Age	.48941	1.000							
Grow	-.0507	-.1823	1.000						
Bond	-.0951	.20423	.05997	1.000					
Disper	.16998	.17132	-.0289	-.1092	1.000				
Fin	.06233	.11145	.00950	.08860	.05787	1.000			
Frage	.39650	.81140	-.1529	-.1998	.09976	.06011	1.000		
Time	.05633	.04329	.03688	-.0379	-.2031	.27838	.02628	1.000	
Start	.16541	.15909	-.0407	-.1634	.12249	-.0162	.09680	-.0451	1.000

Table 6.3: Logistical Model for All Three Industries Combined

Iterations-5
Log-likelihood -337.619417
Log-likelihood with only a constant term -370.013228
Chi-squared (8) = 64.788 @ Prob = 0.00000

Variable		Hypotheses	Coefficient	Std. Error	T-ratio
Constant			-1.43664	0.32211	-4.4601
H1	Size	Positive	0.00110	0.00034	3.2038
H2	Age	Positive	-0.01076	0.00612	-1.7586
H3	Growth	Positive	0.14427	0.05827	2.4760
H4	Bonding	Negative	-0.50015	0.53495	-0.9349
H5	Dispersion	Positive	0.92468	0.23322	3.9649
Control Variables					
B6	Financing		0.15183	0.21491	0.7065
B7	Time		-0.01844	0.04302	-0.4287
B8	Start Costs		0.00018	0.00010	1.8892

Bold = significant at .10 level

MANAGERIAL IMPLICATIONS

Using the results of the logistic regression analysis, the logits can be translated into probabilities. This is done by evaluating the logistic regression for particular values. The formula for converting logits to probabilities is given below.

(1) $e^{logit} / (1 + e^{logit})$

The result of the formula indicates the probability that the franchisor will seek international franchisees (Menard 1995). The classification tables that were provided with each model predict the probability that the franchisor will internationalize. They show that the accuracy of the models' predictions ranges between 72 percent and 78 percent.

Given particular characteristics of a franchising company, franchisees, franchisors, and portfolio investors can predict the probability of internationalization. This may be important to a franchisee who wants to work for a franchisor with the potential for overseas expansion. Franchisors can evaluate whether they are ready to internationalize by comparing their company characteristics with industry standards. Finally, the decision to internationalize may influence the value of the franchising system. Therefore, portfolio investors can benefit by knowing whether a franchisor has the necessary characteristics to internationalize. Correctly predicting the franchisor's intentions can help investors, franchisors, and prospective franchisees make sound decisions.

The globalization of markets should make entry into a foreign country easier in the future. Huszagh et al. (1992) showed that product/service offering differences was not a discriminating factor between domestic and international franchisors. They attributed this finding to the increasing similarities of consumers across countries. They also argued that the globalization of capital markets has increased the efficiency of capital world-wide. As the world becomes smaller through improved technology and communications, and consumer tastes converge, internationalization would become a possibility, and perhaps even a necessity. Market saturation and lower rates of growth in the service economies of most developed countries may make opportunities in less developing countries more appealing. Franchisors that have a distinct market niche and a business strategy that exploits their advantages could become successful in developed and developing market economies across the world.

CONCLUSIONS

This study makes two major contributions. First, it finds that organizational explanations are collectively significant factors of international franchising for all three industries. Particularly, size is positively and significantly related to the decision of franchisors to internationalize. However, this study also finds that the effect of organizational variables on the internationalization of franchisors is industry-specific. This is shown both by the variance in results with respect to significance and the impact of the studied variables. The chow test clearly indicated that the structure of the empirical models was different for the three industrial sectors.

This study is a step in the direction of fulfilling the need for more empirical research. A theoretical model which explains the internationalization of US franchise systems using resource-based and agency perspectives is developed and then tested for three industries: (1) retailing, (2) hotel, and (3) professional business service industries. The results provide strong evidence that organizational factors, or company specific variables, can differentiate between domestic and international franchisors within each industry. Environmental variables such as market saturation and host-country variables cannot explain why some franchisors within each industry internationalize while others stay in the home country. Therefore, this study contributes to the international franchising literature by highlighting the important company variables that influence the decision of franchisors to seek franchisees in foreign markets.

The models in this study were largely consistent with expectations. The sign of all the coefficients, except for the age variable, confirmed the hypotheses. The size of the franchisor, measured as the total number of outlets, was significant for all three models. This shows that economies of scale, experience, and other resources, as well as market saturation may contribute to the internationalization of the service subsectors. The remaining variables were not confirmed by one or more of the models. This may be a result of data deficiencies and substantive differences in the structure of the industries. Despite the insignificance of these variables on an industry basis, the coefficients confirmed the predicted sign hypothesized in this study for all three industries, except for the age variable.

The age of the firm was insignificant for the hotel and professional business service categories, and negatively related to the decision to internationalize for the retailing sector. This is supported by Carney and Gedajlovic's (1991) research that showed that some young companies are highly aggressive, seeking international franchisees early in their life cycle. However, the results for the age variable were non-intuitive from a resource-based perspective. The resource-based approach suggests that the older the firm, the more resources it will have and, therefore, the more likely it is to seek international franchisees. The results in this study show that the sign of the coefficients vary across industry and is negative and significant for the retailing sector.

Although many franchisors attempt to internationalize early in their life cycles, their probability of succeeding may be different from firms that are older and more experienced. Shane (1996a) found that most franchising firms fail within the first 10 years of operation. The effect of age on the success in international ventures shows potential as a future research avenue.

This study also suggests that international franchising investigations, and perhaps all franchising research, should be conducted on an industry-by-industry basis. This suggestion is supported by the chi-squared test of the log-likelihood ratio, the different results obtained for the significance of the coefficients in the different models, and the variations in the contextual variables.

Finally, the models show that the agency perspective could also provide justification for internationalization. While all the models showed the expected signs in the bonding and dispersion variables, both the retailing and the hotel sectors showed significance in one of these variables. These results are consistent with Shane's (1996b) findings that agency theory may help explain the internationalization of US franchising systems.

FUTURE RESEARCH

This study provides evidence that the determinants of international franchising should be investigated at the industry level. Future research should concentrate on other industries to allow for a greater base of comparison.

Second, this study focuses on the organizational determinants of international franchising. More empirical research is needed on the environmental causes of international expansion. Host-country factors influencing international franchising were delineated in Chapter Two. The causal relationships between these factors and the number of international franchisors in the host country should be established. Alon and McKee (1999) have begun to develop a conceptual framework for the environmental factors of international franchising. This would allow researchers to develop a comprehensive model for the internationalization of franchisors which includes organizational and environmental determinants.

Third, the dependent variable used in this study was limited because it was measured categorically. This means that the null hypothesis may not be rejected when in fact it should be (Demaris 1992). An interval-level dependent variable, which for example would measure the number of foreign outlets or the number of countries in which the franchisor operated, would provide more information. This has the potential to change the significance of the results of the analyses. Furthermore, by knowing the number of international outlets, the effect of the size variable can be determined more accurately. This is because the researcher will be able to focus on the effect of the number of domestic franchise outlets on the decision to internationalize. Therefore, future research should attempt to seek interval-level dependent variables for the number of international outlets for each franchisor.

Finally, the proxies that were employed in this study have been previously used in the franchising literature to represent the resources and monitoring capabilities of the franchise firm. However, better proxies may be developed for resources and monitoring capabilities. Future research can focus on methods for improving the measurement of the independent and dependent variables.

It is hoped that future studies will review the results obtained in this study in order to further facilitate the understanding of the internationalization process on franchising systems. A promising research avenue is to develop a conceptual model which will incorporate both the organizational and environmental determinants of international franchising. This should be followed by a research agenda to test this model. Such a development will make a major contribution to an understanding of the internationalization of franchise systems around the world.

Bibliography

Ackerman, KID., D. E. Bush, and R. T. Justis (1994), "Determinants of Internationalization of Franchise Operations by US Franchisors," *International Marketing Review*, 11 (no. 4), 56–68.

Aharoni, Yair (1966), *The Foreign Direct Investment Decision Process*. Boston, Mass.: Harvard University Press.

Akehurst, Gary and Nicholas Alexander (1995), "A Conceptual Model of Strategic Considerations for International Retail Expansion," in *The Internationalisation of Retailing*, Gary Akenhurst and Nicholas Alexander, eds., Frank Cass, London, 1–15.

Aliber, R. A. (1975), "Exchange Risk, Political Risk and Investor Demands for External Currency Deposits," *Journal of Money, Credit and Banking*, 7, 161–179.

Alon, Ilan and David McKee (1999), "Towards a Macro Environmental Model of International Franchising," *Multinational Business Review*, 7 (2), 76–82.

Alon, Ilan (1998), "A Conceptual Model of the Internationalization of the United States Franchising Systems," in *Business Research Yearbook: Global Business Perspectives*, Jerry Biberman and Abbass Alkhafaji, eds., The International Academy of Business Disciplines, Michigan, 350–355.

Alon, Ilan (1997), "The Association Between Political Risk and International Franchising Mode of Entry," in *Expanding Marketing Horizons into the 21st Century*, David L. Moore, eds., Association of Marketing Theory and Practice, Jekyll Island, South Carolina, 433–440.

Arthur Andersen (1995), *Worldwide Franchising Statistics: A Study of Worldwide Franchise Associations*. Arthur Andersen and Co., SC. in cooperation with the World Franchising Council.

Arthur Andersen (1996), *International Expansion by U.S. Franchisors*. Arthur Andersen LLP Chicago, Illinois in cooperation with the International Franchise Association, Washington, DC.

Ascher, W. (1982), "Political Forecasting: The Missing Link," *Journal of Forecasting*, 1, 227–239.

Aulakh, S. Preet, and Masaaki Kotabe (1993), "An Assessment of Theoretical and Methodological Development in International Marketing: 1980–1990." *Journal of International Marketing*, 1 , 5–28.

Aydin, N. and M. Kacker (1990), "International Outlook on US-Based Franchisors," *International Marketing Review*, 7 (2), 206–219.

Basi, R. S. (1963), *Determinants of United States Private Direct Investment*. Kent, Ohio: Kent State University.

Bass, B. M., D. W. McGregor and J. L. Walters (1977), "Selecting Foreign Plant Sites: Economic, Social, and Political Considerations," *Academy of Management Journal*, 4. 535–551.

Bennett, D. Peter, and Robert T. Green (1972), "Political Instability as a Determinant of Direct Foreign Investment in Marketing," *Journal of Marketing Research*, 9 (May), 182–186.

Bergen, M., S. Dutta, and O. C. Walker (1992), "Agency Relationships in Marketing: A Review of the Implication and Application of Agency and Related Theories," *Journal of Marketing*, (July), 1–24.

Boddewyn, J. J., B. M. Halbrich, and C. A. Perry (1986), "Service Multinationals: Conceptualization, Measurement and Theory," *Journal of International Business Studies*, (Fall), 41–57.

Brickley, J. A., and F. H. Dark (1987), "The Choice of Organizational Form: The Case of Franchising," *Journal of Financial Economics*, 18 (2), 401–420.

Brickley, J. A., and M. S. Weisbach (1991), "An Agency Perspective on Franchising," *Financial Management*, 20 (1), 27–35.

Burton, F. N., and A. R. Cross (1995), "Franchising and Foreign Market Entry," in *International Marketing Reader*, S. J. Paliwoda and J. K. Ryans, eds., London: Routledge, 35–48.

Carney, M., and E. Gedajlovic (1991), "Vertical Integration in Franchising Systems: Agency Theory and Resource Explanations, *Strategic Management Journal*, 12 (8), 607–629.

Castrogiovanni, Gary J., Robert T. Justis, and Scott Julian (1993), "Franchise Failure Rates: An Assessment of Magnitude and Influencing Factors" *Journal of Small Business Management*, 31 (2), 105–114.

Castrogiovanni, H. J., N. Bennett, and J. G. Combs (1995), "Franchisor Types: Reexamination and Clarification," *Journal of Small Business Management*, 33 (1), 45–55.

Caves, R. E., and W. F. Murphy (1976), "Franchising: Firms, Markets, and Intangible Assets," *Southern Economic Journal*, 42 (4), 572–586.

Combs, James G., and Gary J. Castrogiovanni (1994), "Franchisor Strategy: A Proposed Model and Empirical Rest of Franchise Versus Company Ownership," *Journal of Small Business Management*, 32 (2), 37–48.

Committee on Small Business (1990), "Franchising in the US Economy: Hearing," *Government Printing Office*, Washington DC.

Conner, K. R. (1991), "A Historical Comparison of Resource-Based Theory and Five Schools of Thought Within Industrial Organizational Economics: Do We Have a New Theory of the Firm," *Journal of Management*, 17 (1), 121–154.

Cross, James C., and Bruce J. Walker (1987), "Service Marketing and Franchising: A Practical Business Marriage," *Business Horizons*, 30 (6), 50–58.

Daniels, P. W. (1993), *Service Industries in the World Economy*, Blackwell Publishers, Cambridge, Massachusetts.

Davies, Keri, and Fergus Fergusson (1995), "A Conceptual Model of Strategic Considerations for International Retail Expansion," in *The Internationalisation of Retailing*, Gary Akenhurst and Nicholas Alexander, eds., Frank Cass, London, 97–117.

Demaris, Alfred (1992), *Logit Modeling: Practical Applications*, Newbury Park, CA: Sage Publications.

Dess, Gregory and Alex Miller (1993), *Strategic Management*, New York: McGraw-Hill, Inc.

Drake, R. L. , and A. J. Prager (1977), "Floundering with Foreign Investment Planning," *Columbia Journal of World Business*, 12 (2), 66–77.

Dubin, Robert (1978), *Theory Building* (Revised Edition), New York: Free Press.

Eitman D. K., A. I. Stonehill, and M. H. Moffett (1991), *Multinational Business Finance*, Massachusetts: Addison-Wesley Publishing Company.

Eroglu, Sevgin (1992), "The Internationalization Process of Franchise Systems: A Conceptual Model," *International Marketing Review*, 9 (5), 19–30.

Falbe, Cecilia M., and Thomas C. Dandridge (1992), "Franchising as a Strategic Partnership: Issues of Cooperation and Conflict in a Global Market," *International Small Business Journal*, 10 (3), 40–52.

Farmer, Richard N. (1973), "Looking Back at Looking Forward," *Business Horizons*, (February), 21–28.

Fatehi-Sadeh, K. and M. Safizadeh (1988), "Sociological Events and Foreign Direct Investments in South and Central American Countries, 1950–1982," *Journal of Management*, 14, 93–107.

Fatehi-Sadeh, K. and M. Safizadeh (1989), "The Association Between Political Instability and Flow of Foreign Direct Investment," *Management International Review*, 29 (4), 4–13.

Fatehi-Sadeh, K. and M. Safizadeh (1994), "The Effect of Sociopolitical Instability on the Flow of Different Types of Foreign Direct Investment," *Journal of Business Research*, 31 (1), 65–73.

Feketekuty, Geza (1988), *International Trade in Services: An Overview and Blueprint for Negotiations*, American Enterprise Institute, Washington D.C.

Fitzpatrick, Mark (1983), "The Definition and Assessment of Political Risk in International Business: A Review of the literature," *Academy of Management Review*, 8 (2), 249–254.

Fladmoe-Lindquist, Karin (1996), "International Franchising: Capabilities and Development," *Journal of Business Venturing*, 11 (5), 419–438.

Fladmoe-Lindquist, Karin, and Laurent L. Jacque (1995), "Control Modes in International Service Operations: The Propensity to Franchise," *Management Science*, 41 (July), 1238–1249.

Franchise Opportunities Handbook (1994), *US Department of Commerce Minority Business Development Agency*, (October), Washington, D.C.

Green, R. T. and C. M. Smith (1972), "Multinational Profitability as a Function of Political Instability," *Management International Review*, 5 (2/3), 23–29.

Gujarati, Damodar N. (1995), *Basic Econometrics* (Third Edition), New York: McGraw-Hill, Inc.

Hackett, D. W. (1976), The International Expansion of US Franchise Systems: Status and Strategies," *Journal of International Business Studies*, 7 (Spring), 66–75.

Haendel and West (1975), *Overseas Investment and Political Risk*. Philadelphia: Foreign Policy Institute.

Hair, Joseph F., Ralph E. Andersen, Ronald L. Tatham, and William C. Black (1992), *Multivariate Data Analysis with Readings* (Third Edition). New York: Macmillan Publishing Company.

Haner, F. T. (1979), "Rating Investment Risks Abroad," *Business Horizons*, 22 (2), 18–23.

Hashmi, Mohammad A. (1987), "Political Risk Assessment in US Multinational Corporations: An Analysis of the Utilization of Political Risk Assessment Models," *Unpublished Dissertation*, Kent State University.

Hoffman, Richard C., John F. Preble (1991), "Franchising: Selecting a Strategy for Rapid Growth," *Long Range Planning*, 24(No 4), 74–85.

Hunt, Shelbe D. (1973), "The Trend Toward Company-Operated Units in Franchise Chains," *Journal of Retailing*, 49 (2), 3–11.

Hunt, S. D. and J. R. Nevin (1975), "Tying Agreements in Franchising," *Journal of Marketing*, 39 (July), 20–26.

Huszagh, S. M., F. W. Huszagh, and F. McIntyre (1992) "International Franchising in the Context of Competitive Strategy and the Theory of the Firm," *International Marketing Review*, 9 (5), 5–18.

Judge, George G., William E. Griffith, R. Carter Hill, and Tsoung-Chao Lee (1980), *The Theory and Practice of Econometrics*, New York: John Wiley and Sons.

Juhl, P. (1985), "Economically Rational Design of Developing Countries Expropriation Policies toward Foreign Direct Investment," *Management International Review*, 25, 44–52.

Justis R. and R. Judd (1986), "Master Franchising: A New Look," *Journal of Small Business Management*, 24 (3), 16–21.

Justis R. and R. Judd (1989), *Franchising*, Cincinnati: South-Western publishing Co.

Kedia, Ben L., David J. Ackerman, Donna E. Bush, and Robert T. Justice (1994), "Determinants of Internationalization of Franchise

Operations by US Franchisors," *International Marketing Review*, 11 (4), 56–66.

Kobrin, Stephen J. (1979), "Political Risk: A Review and Reconsideration's," *Journal of International Business Studies*, 44 (Spring), 32–47.

Kobrin, Stephen J. (1976), "The Environmental Determinants of Foreign Direct Manufacturing Investment: An Ex-Post Empirical Analysis," *Journal of International Business*, 2 (Fall/Winter), 29–42.

Kostecka, Andrew (1969 -1988), "Franchising in the Economy," *US Department of Commerce*, Washington D.C.

LaFontaine, F. (1992), "Agency Theory and Franchising: Some Empirical Results," *Rand Journal of Econometrics*, 23 (2), 263–283.

LaFontaine, Francine and Patrick J. Kaufmann (1994), " The Evolution of Ownership Patterns in Franchise Systems," *Journal of Retailing*, 70 (2), 97–114.

Lester, Digman A. (1990), *Strategic Management* (Second Edition), Homewood, IL: BPI Irwin.

Love, John F. (1995), *McDonald's Behind the Arches*, New York: Bantam Books.

Martin, R. (1988), "Franchising and Risk Management," *American Economic Review*, 78 (5), 954–968.

Martin, R., and Justis R. (1993), "Franchising, Liquidity Constraints and Entry," *Applied Economics*, 25 (9), 1269–1277.

McClendon, McKee J. (1994), *Multiple Regression and Causal Analysis*, F.E. Peacock Publishers, Illinois.

Menard, Scott (1995), *Applied Logistic Regression Analysis*, Thousand Oaks, California: Sage Publications.

Mendelshon, Martin (1994), "International Franchising — the Financial Dilemma," *Franchising World*, 26 (Sep/Oct), 62.

Nigh, Douglas (1985), "The Effect of Political Events on US Direct Foreign Investment: A Pooled Time Series Cross-sectional Analysis," *Journal of International Business*, 16 (Spring), 1–17.

Norton, S. (1988), "An Empirical Look at Franchising as an Organizational Form," *Journal of Business*, 61, 197–217.

Noyelle, Thierry J., and Anna B. Dutka (1988), *International Trade in Business Services*, American Enterprise Institute, Washington D.C.

Oseghale, Braimoh D. (1993), *Political Instability, Interstate Conflict, Adverse Changes in Host Government Policies and Foreign Direct Investment: A Sensitivity Analysis*, New York: Garland Publishing.

Oxenfeldt, Alferd R., and Anthony O. Kelly (1969), "Will Successful Franchise Systems Ultimately Become Wholly-Owned Chains?," *Journal of Retailing*, 44, 69–87.

Pan, Yigang (1996), Influences on Foreign Equity Ownership Level in Joint Ventures in China," *Journal of International Business Studies*, 1–26.

Phillips-Patrick, F. J. (1991), "Political Risk and Organizational Form," *Journal of Law and Economics*, 34 (October), 675–93.

Pollio, G. and C. H. Riemenschneider (1988), "The Coming Third World Investment Revival," *Harvard Business Review*, 66, 114–124.

Rice, Gillian and Essam Mahmoud (1990), "Political Risk Forecasting by Canadian Firms," *International Journal of Forecasting*, 6, 89–102.

Robock, Stefan H. (1971), "Political Risk: Identification and Assessment," *Columbia Journal of World Business*, 6 (July/August), 6–20.

Rubin, P. (1978), "The Theory of the Firm and the Structure of the Franchise Contract," *Journal of Law and Economics*, 21, 223–234.

Root, Franklin R. (1972), "Analyzing Political Risks in International Business," in *The Multinational Enterprise Transition*, edited by A. Dapoor and Philip D. Grub, Princeton: Darwin Press, 354–365.

Root, Franklin R. (1987), *Entry Strategies for International Markets*. Mass.: Lexington Books.

Rubel, Chad (1995), "Franchising Fellowship," *Marketing Management*, 4 (No 2), 4–6.

Rubin, Paul (1978), "The Theory of the Firm and Structure of the Franchise System," *Journal of Law and Economics*, 21 (April), 222–223.

Rummel, R. J. and D. A. Heenan (1978), "How Multinationals Analyze Political Risk," *Harvard Business Review*, 56 (1), 67–76.

Schollhammer, H. and D. Nigh (1984), "The Effect of Political Events on Foreign Direct Investment by German Multinational Corporations," *International Management Review*, 24, 18–40.

Sethi, Prakash S. and K. A. N. Luther (1986), "Political Risk Analysis and Direct Foreign Investment: Some Problems of Definition and

Measurement," *California Management Review*, 28, (Winter), 57–68.

Shane, S. (1996a), "Hybrid Organizational Arrangements and Their Implications For Firm Growth And Survival: A Study of New Franchisors," *Academy of Management Journal*, 39 (1), 216–234.

Shane, S. (1996b), "Why Franchise Companies Expand Overseas," *Journal of Business Venturing*, 11 (2), 73–88.

Shreeve, Thomas W. (1984), "Be Prepared for Political Changes Abroad," *Harvard Business Review*, ? (July/August), 111–118.

Simon, J. D. (1982), "Political Risk Assessment: Past Trends and Future Prospects," *Columbia Journal of World Business*, (Fall), 62–71.

Simpson, Eithel M., and Dayle I. Thorpe (1995) "A Conceptual Model of Strategic Considerations for International Retail Expansion," in *The Internationalisation of Retailing*, Gary Akenhurst and Nicholas Alexander, eds., Frank Cass, London, 16–24.

Stanworth, John, and Thomas Dandridge (1994), "Business Franchising and Economic Change: An Overview," *International Small Business Journal*, 12 (2), 12–14.

Stapenhurst, Fredrick (1992), *Political Risk Analysis Around the North Atlantic*. London: MacMillan Press LTD.

Steinberg, Carol (1992), "International Franchising: Signs of the Times," *World Trade*, 5 (Aug/Sep), 110–113.

Stobaugh, Robert B. (1969), "How to Analyze Foreign Investment Climates," *Harvard Business Review*, 6 (September/October), 100–108.

Tallman, Stephen B. (1988), "Home Country Political Risk and Foreign Direct Investment in the United States," *Journal of International Business Studies*, ? (Summer), 221–234.

Ting, Wenlee (1988), *Multinational Risk Assessment and Management*. New York: Quorum Books.

Torre, Jose de la, and David H. Neckar (1988), "Forecasting Political Risks for International Operations," *International Journal of Forecasting*, 4, 221–241.

Trankiem, Luu (1979), "International Franchising: A Way to Capture Foreign Markets," *Los Angeles Business and Economics*, 4 (Summer/Fall), 26–30.

Tucker, Ken, and Mark Sundberg (1988), *International Trade in Services*, Billing and Sons Ltd, Worchester, Great Britain.

Van Agtmeal, A. (1976), "How Business Has Dealt with Political Risk," *Financial Executive*, 44, 26–30.

Vernon, Raymond (1966), "International Investment and International Trade in the Product Cycle," *Quarterly Journal of Economics*, 30 (May), 190–207.

Walker, J. B., and Michael J. Etzel (1973), "The Internationalization of US Franchise Systems: Progress and Procedures," *Journal of Marketing*, 37, 38–46.

Welch, Lawrence S. (1989), "Diffusion of Franchise Systems Use in International Operations," *International Marketing Review*, 6 (5), 7–19.

Whitehead, Maureen (1991), "International Franchising — Marks & Spencer: A Case Study," *International Journal of Retail and Distribution Management*, 19 (2), 10–12.

Yavas, Burhan F., and Demos Vardiabasis (1987), "The Determinants of US International Fast Food Franchising: An Application of the Pacific Basin" Proceedings of the *Academy of Marketing Science*, 10 (11), 161–164.

Zeidman, P.F. (1992), "International Franchising: It Works Both Ways," *Franchising World* 24 (1), 46–47.

Index

Age, 28–29, 69–70
  See also Independent Variables
Agency Theories, 23, **29–32**, 52–
  53, 57
Australia, 21–22
Business Format Franchising, 11–
  12
Canada, 21
Control Variables, 32–33, 40–41,
  53, 57, 64–65
Data
  See Entrepreneur
Dependent Variable
  See Intention to Internationalize
Direct Investment, 13
Dispersion
  See Geographical Dispersion
Domestic Market Saturation, 22
Entrepreneur, 7–8, 37
Exporting, 13
Financing
  See Control Variables
Franchise Life Cycle Theory, 21–
  22
Franchising
  and Services, 3
Future Research 77–79

Geographical Dispersion, 31–32,
  71–72
  See also Independent Variables
Growth Rate
  See Rate of Growth
Growth
  See Rate of Growth
Hotel and Motel Sector, 54–58
Hypotheses, 6–7, 38, 67–72
  See Also Independent Variables
Independent Variables, 26–33, 39–
  40,
Industry
  See Control Variables
Intention to Internationalize, 39
International Franchising
  Definitions, 12–14
• Theories, 14–16
  Environmental Factors of, 16–
  21
  Organizational Factors of, 21–
  24
Japan, 21
Licensing, 12–13
Logistic Regression
  Rational, 43
  Theory, 44

Interpretation, 44–45
Managerial Implications, 75–76
Master Franchising, 22
Methodology, 7–8
Number of Outlets
    See Size
Organization of the Study, 8–9
Price bonding, 30–31, 70–71
    See Also Independent Variables
Product/trade-name, 11
Professional Business Services
    Sector, 58–65
Rate of Growth, 29–30, 69–70
    See also Independent Variables
Regression
    See Logistic Regression
Research Design, 6,
Research Hypotheses
    See Hypotheses
Research Questions, 6

Resource-Based Theories, 23, 26–29, 52, 57, 63–64
Retailing Sector, 48–54
Robustness
    Retailing, 53
    Hotels and Motels, 57–58
    Professional Business Services, 65
Shane, Scott, 5
Size, 27–28, 69
    See also Independent Variables
Start-Up Costs
    See Control Variables
Statistical Method
    See Logistic Regression
Structure of Coefficients, 72
Time
    See Control Variables
United Kingdom, 21–22

About the Author

Ilan Alon (Ph.D., Kent State University) is Assistant Professor of International Business and Marketing at the State University of New York Oneonta. His research interests are in the areas of international franchising theory, political risk assessment, and regional developments in the Middle-East and East Asia. His publications have appeared in international business and marketing journals such as *Journal of Global Business, Multinational Business Review, and Journal of Consumer Marketing*, as well as refereed conference proceedings such as Academy of International Business, World Business Congress, International Society of Franchising and International Academy of Business Studies.